Third Eye Chakra

Healing Therapy, Fundamentals of Chakra Balance

Energy Academy

© Copyright 2019 - All rights reserved.

This Book is provided with the sole purpose of providing relevant information on a specific topic for which every reasonable effort has been made to ensure that it is both accurate and reasonable. Nevertheless, by purchasing this Book you consent to the fact that the author, as well as the publisher, are in no way experts on the topics contained herein, regardless of any claims as such that may be made within. As such, any suggestions or recommendations that are made within are done so purely for entertainment value. It is recommended that you always consult a professional prior to undertaking any of the advice or techniques discussed within.

This is a legally binding declaration that is considered both valid and fair by both the Committee of Publishers Association and the American Bar Association and should be considered as legally binding within the United States.

The reproduction, transmission, and duplication of any of the content found herein, including any specific or extended information will be done as an illegal act regardless of the end form the information ultimately takes. This includes copied versions of the work both physical, digital, and audio unless express consent of the

Publisher is provided beforehand. Any additional rights reserved.

Furthermore, the information that can be found within the pages described forthwith shall be considered both accurate and truthful when it comes to the recounting of facts. As such, any use, correct or incorrect, of the provided information will render the Publisher free of responsibility as to the actions taken outside of their direct purview. Regardless, there are zero scenarios where the original author or the Publisher can be deemed liable in any fashion for any damages or hardships that may result from any of the information discussed herein.

Additionally, the information in the following pages is intended only for informational purposes and should thus be thought of as universal. As befitting its nature, it is presented without assurance regarding its prolonged validity or interim quality. Trademarks that are mentioned are done without written consent and can in no way be considered an endorsement from the trademark holder.

TABLE OF CONTENTS

Introduction 11
Chapter 1 What Is Energy Healing 14
    History 15
    Beliefs 16
    Scientific Investigation 18
        Detached Healing 18
        Contact Healing 19
        Evidence-Base 19
        Classification of Energy Healing 21
Chapter 2 Types of Energy Healing 24
    Sound Healing Therapy 24
        Types of Sound Therapy 25
        Vibroacoustic Therapy 25
        Guided Meditation 25
        Bonny Method 26
        Nordoff-Robbins 26
        Singing Bowl Therapy 26
        Brainwave Entertainment 27
        Turning Fork Therapy 27
        How Sound Healing Works 28
        Benefits of Sound Healing 28
        Instruments Used in Sound Healing 28
        Touch therapy 29
        Reiki 29
        About Reiki 29
        Techniques Used in Reiki 30
        Happenings in Reiki Sessions 31
        Health Benefits 31

Safety of Reiki 34
Where to Get Reiki 35
How to be a Reiki Practitioner and Regulations 36
Therapeutical Touch 37
Researched Evidence 39
How TT Works 41
Happenings in TT Session 42
Assessment 42
Intervention 43
Assessment/conclusion 43
Health Benefits of TT 43
Lupus 44
Safety of TT 45
How to Become a TT Practitioner 45
ETF 46
Advantages of ETF 47
Diet Desires 47
Acupuncture 48
Clinical Research 51
Needles 54
Needle Techniques Insertion 55
De-qi 55
Related Searches 56
Efficiency 59
Publication Bias 62
Pain 63
Lower Back Pain 65
Headaches and Migraine 67
Expectations in Session 69

Risks 70
How to Find a Practitioner 70
Crystal Healing 71
Scientific Evidence 73
Qigong 74
Benefits of Qigong 76
Safety and Cost 76
Intuitive Healing 77
How It Works 77
The Secret Behind 78
The Role of an Intuitive Healing Practitioner—Witnessing 79
The Seven Elevations of Consciousness 80
12 Strand DNA and DNA Activation 80
Clear Negative Energy 81
Manifesting Abundance 82
Guardian Angels, Spirit Guides and the Deceased 82
One Path Many Ways to Apply 82
Spiritual Healing 83
The Journey of Spiritual Healing 83
Do Your Body Right 84
Sleep 84
Purify Your Relationship 85
Use the Mind for Creative Freedom 85
Commence the Spiritual Trip 87
Magnetic Field Therapy 88
Static Magnetic Field Therapy 89
Its Workings 89
Uses 90
Polarity Therapy 91

Benefits of Polarity Healing 93

How It Works 93

Safety 95

Research and Acceptance 95

Practitioner 96

Chakra 96

Root Chakra What It Is 97

When It Is Blocked 98

The Sacral Chakra What Is It 98

When It Is Blocked 98

The Solar Plexus Chakra What Is It 99

When It Is Blocked 99

The Heart Chakra What It Is 99

When It Is Blocked 100

Throat Chakra What It Is 100

When It Is Blocked 101

The Third Eye Chakra What Is It 101

When It Is Blocked 101

The Crown Chakra What Is It 102

When It Is Blocked 102

How to Unlock Chakra 103

Mantra 103

Select a Mantra 103

How to Use Mantra When Meditating 105

Tapping 105

Tapping Chakra Points 105

Reiki 106

How Reiki Unlocks 106

Yoga 107

- Blocked Chakra 107
- Learning How to Unblock A Chakra 107
- Chapter 3 More About Energy Healing 108
  - Benefits of Energy Healing 108
    - Better Stress Management 109
    - Better Self-care 110
    - Better Relationships 110
    - Better Creativity and Productivity 111
    - Better Ease and Happiness 112
    - Better Real Life Magic and Manifestation 113
    - Emotional let loose and curative 114
    - Balancing of energy 114
    - Energy Remedial 114
    - Healing Energy is Grounded on Scientific Philosophies ... 115
    - Healing Energy Is Absolutely Available 117
    - Your Energetic Health Can Be Maintained at Home 118
    - Reasons to Try Energy Healing 118
    - Clears mental thought and negative emotional patterns. ... 120
    - How It Works 121
    - Black Magic 121
    - Basics of Energy Healing 122
    - Attunement/Initiation 123
    - Physical Presence and Remote Healing 125
    - They Need a Pickup 126
    - Where Does the Energy Come From? 127
    - How Does the Healing Really Work? 129
    - Healing Hurts 131
    - What You Get in Exchange 131
    - Receiving Negative Energy from Others 132

    Symbols 133

   Intermediate Level 134

    Breath work 134

    Grounding 134

    Attention to Energy Flow.. 134

    Love and Intuition 135

    Looping Through the Rainbow 135

    Structures, Clouds, Bandages 136

    Masculine and Feminine Energies.. 136

    Advanced 137

    Implants, Bids and Gags... 138

    Parasites 141

    The Mind Is the Body and The Body Is the Mind 142

    Super Complex Stuff... 144

Chapter 4 Fundamentals of Chakra Balance 147

Chapter 5 The Root Chakra 150

   Root Chakra Blockage... 152

   How To Heal The Root Chakra 153

Chapter 6 The Sacral Chakra 157

   Symptoms of an Unhealthy Sacral Chakra............................... 158

   Sacral Chakra Blockage... 159

   Healing Sacral Chakra 160

Chapter 7 The Solar plexus.. 164

   Symptoms of an Unhealthy Solar Plexus 165

   Solar Plexus Blockage 166

   Healing the Solar Plexus 166

Chapter 8 The Heart Chakra.. 171

   Symptoms of an Unhealthy Heart Chakra 172

   How to Heal your Heart Chakra 174

Chapter 9 The Throat chakra 180
    Throat Chakra Blockage 183
    Healing of the Throat Chakra 184
Chapter 10 Third Eye Chakra 192
    Symptoms of an Unhealthy Third Eye Chakra 194
    Third Eye Chakra Blockage 196
    Healing the Third Eye Chakra 198
Chapter 11 The Crown Chakra 207
    Symptoms of Unhealthy of the Crown Chakra 209
    Apathy 209
    Insomnia 209
    Chronic fatigue 209
    A deficient or overactive Crown Chakra 210
    Healing the Crown Chakra 211
Chapter 12 Benefits of Chakra Balance 220
Chapter 13 Radiate Positive Energy 229
    50 Ways to radiate positive energy 230
Conclusion 246

Introduction

Energy healing—we might be asking ourselves what this is. Well, you picked the right book. We are going to discuss energy healing in detail as we progress in this book. Energy healing has been in

everyone's discussion of late. Although it is something that has always been there, people have always just shrugged about it, and it is only until recently that it has been embraced. It has existed for centuries. It is that we are only beginning to embrace this is a way of healing now as westerners and easterners who thought it was uncivilized to practice such and backward to use energy healing instead of modern medicine. Energy healing has now been embarrassed by people all over the world, do not be left out as we are going to discuss everything about energy healing. Energy healing will change your life, with energy healing your body gets rejuvenated, and you get a sense of healing.

Energy healing might be ancient, but it still works magic to date. Ever wondered why people during the past used to have a long lifespan? Well, this is because they used to practice healthy ways of living. They would facilitate the well-being of the body through energy healing, bringing about a natural healing of the body and without much stress, they would live more years than we do nowadays because we always have stress from everything around us. We are surrounded by stressful situations, and just getting rid of them could be key to some more years, and energy healing is just the right thing to help in stress-relieving. Why don't you also try out this method of healing and also experience the magic of energy healing the good thing is its completely natural. The first step to this is reading through this to know more as we all know knowledge is power, and this book could be all the power you will need to know about energy healing. By the time you are done going through it, you will be for sure more knowledgeable and know exactly where to go to, what to expect, and the best method that could work well for you.

In this book, we are going to take you through energy healing discussing in detail, what energy healing is, the types of energy healing this will give you an insight of every type we will discuss the benefits of energy healing and more about energy healing that we have not always known. This book could be the beginning of your beautiful life ahead because with energy healing life is beautiful. Your first step to a healthy life is by learning the facts about energy healing before starting to join the millions of people who are now living a happy life due to energy healing. Get on board and read through this; you will not be disappointed.

Chapter 1 What Is Energy Healing

Energy healing, also known as energy medicine, is a method of restoring or balancing the energy zones of the body in order to improve health by delivering energy healing through the hands of

doctors to the patient's body. Therapy of energy healing is used to cure several ailments. There are many techniques for an energy treatment, including the palm, arms, and distance healing, that the healer and the clients are not in the same locations. Fascinatingly, 57 percent of long-term treatment trials showed a positive treatment effect on each disease.

There are many schools of energy healing that use many names, such as healing biologically, healing spiritually, healing by contact, healing in the street healing, qido, sensory therapy, Reiki or qigong. Do not think of traditional religious beliefs as a condition of healing. Unlike faith, healing is done in the context of traditional religion. Previous reviews of the literature science behind healing energy are categorical furthermore recommend further research, but the latest analyses have established that there is zero proof of clinical efficiency. The hypothetical foundations of therapeutic are criticized as irrational, the studies and evaluations that underlie energy therapy are responsible for the content of methodological defects and dysfunctions, and a positive therapeutic result is determined by well-known psychological mechanisms. The alternative drug at the University of Exeter said: "Despite the lack of biological validity or convincing clinical data, treatment is still encouraged. These methods are enough to prove that they are therapeutic, not." Some of these allegations are known as "energy medicine" device fraud, and judicial practice is being prosecuted in the United States.

History

History captures a recurring relationship or the use of scientific discoveries by those who claim that the newly learned science can aid people in recovering. Back in the 19th century, magnetism and also electricity and which were the "innovations" of science, and the shamanism of electricity grew. These concepts motivate authors in the New Age movement. At the beginning of the 20th era, claims about the health hazards of radioactive materials were life-threatening, and in recent years, the quantum method and also fusion concept have provided chances for marketable use on a large scale. Thousands of devices are used that claim to be cured of energy used or estimated worldwide. Many people sell with statements that are illegal or dangerous, false, or unproven. Some of these devices are prohibited. From the point of view of energetic and also spiritual healing, this is linked with severe injuries or deaths in case the patients stop or cancel a treatment.

Beliefs

Energy healing depends on the confidence of the patient and the doctor in the doctor's ability to direct healing energy in various ways to those who want help, for example, in hands, arms and remote (or absent) positions. Practitioners say that this "healing energy" sometimes seems warm to therapists. There are many types of energy healing, including biomedical energy healing, spiritual healing, contact healing, distance healing, qi-do, sensory therapy, Reiki, qigong, and much more. Spiritual healing is largely non-religious. Traditional religious beliefs are not considered a prerequisite for healing. On the contrary, healing of faith takes place in a religious context. Energy medicine experts often refer to ministries, but they are not a "cure or death" practice.

Healing energy methods, for instance, Touch of Therapeutics, has been recognized in nurse's work. In the years between 2005-2006, The North American Associations of Nurses has confirmed the diagnosis of "energy field disorder" in patients, reflecting a different approach called "postmodern" or "anti-scientific" treatment. This approach is very important. The followers of these techniques provide a mysterious quantum appeal to non-local ones to explain remote healing. They also suggest that the therapist acts as a channel for delivering biomagnetic waves similar to important pseudoscience, for instance, org or qi. Drew Leder, in his article in the Journal of Complementary and Alternative Medicine, notes which the idea is "an attempt to remotely understand, interpret, and study psi and healing." And "physical models are presented as implicit, not explanations." Beverly Rubik relies on his beliefs based on articles in the same journal with reference to biophysics, bioelectromagnetic systems, and chaos theory. James Oshman introduces the concept of healing electromagnetic fields with varying frequency. Oshman had faith that the "healing energy" comes from frequencies of electromagnetic created by therapeutic devices developed by electrons that act as healing hands or antioxidants. Physicists and skeptics criticize this explanation as pseudo physics. Indeed, even those who are passionate about healing energy say: "There is a very narrow theoretical basis on which [spiritual] healing is based."

Scientific Investigation

Detached Healing

An organized review of 23 remote curative studies put out in 2000 was not completed due to the methodological limitations of the study. The year 2001, brought writers of the study, Edward Ernst, wrote a guide to cancer treatment, stating that "approximately half of this research shows that this treatment is effective," "very controversial" and "methodological defects." I did this. "Spiritual healing must be truly risk-free until it is used as an effective alternative," he concluded. In a randomized clinical trial since 2001, no statistically significant difference in chronic pain was found in the same group between the removed therapist3waaaaaaaaq and the "simulated therapist." Ernst's 2003 review, which updated previous work, concluded that the weight of evidence changed to long-term treatment that could be damaged. "

Contact Healing

In a randomized clinical trial conducted in 2001 patients, in approximation, with prolonged pain, were randomly assigned to doctors or "simulated doctors," nevertheless they were unable to demonstrate the effectiveness of the treatment from a distance or face. A systematic review of 2008 showed that evidence of certain effects of mental healing on reducing neuropathy or neuralgia is not conclusive. In a 2008 manuscript, "Trick or Treat," Simon Singh and also Edward Ernst said: "Spiritual healing is biologically irrational, the effect of which depends on the placebo response and, at best, the comfort response. If you have a serious illness that requires first aid."

Evidence-Base

Edward Ernst, an alternative medicine researcher, said that the first review of long-term treatment trials before 1999 positively identified 57% of the study, but subsequent examinations of randomized medical trials were carried out between 2000 and 2002. "The most rigorous studies do not support the hypothesis that there is a specific therapeutic effect for distant treatment," he concluded. Ernst defines the proof base for soothing practices as "very negative." Many reviews also question the lack of data found, transparency, and errors. He concluded: "This is not biological meaning or strong clinical evidence, but spiritual healing continues to advance. This method is therapeutic and sufficient to prove that this is not so. " Quality of life, symptoms of depression, in the 2014 Energy Therapy Study for Colorectal Cancer Patients.

Explanation for Affirmative Feedback

There are many psychosomatic enlightenments for the affirmative information of energy healing, among them are the placebo effect, impulsive remissions, and reasoning dissonance. According to a 2009 analysis, the "small accomplishments" info for the two treatments proposed together as "energy psychology" (breakthrough acupressure and emotive choice techniques) could be caused by known cognitive factors and behavioral factors associated with manipulating energy. Biologists and researchers should carefully use such methods to try to educate the community more of the negative effects of therapy that can lead to unbelievable claims. "

There are twofold treatment accounts or anecdotal descriptions that need not be replaced with bizarre. To begin is initial hoc ergo propter hoc, which means that actual recovery or impulsive palliation can be a coincidence, regardless of the actions or words of the doctor or patient. These patients will recover if they do not do anything. To follow is the placebo outcome that allows one to feel real soreness and other forms of relief. In this case, the easy-going really helps the doctor. This is not mysterious or many functions, but the power of his belief that he will recover. In both cases, even if no miraculous or unexplained events occur, the patient might know- how a marked decrease in signs. In both cases, this is very limited by the body's natural abilities.

The positive results obtained in scientific research can be methodological defects, such as the results of the same psychological mechanism or the results of experimental biases, lack of blindness or bias in the publication. Positive reviews in the scientific literature may indicate bias. Because there are no important studies that do not correspond to the position of the author, in assessing a claim, all these factors must be considered.

Classification of Energy Healing

The word "energy medicine" has existed for the user since the creation of the non-profit international association for the study of excellent energy and energy medicine in the 1980s. This guide is available to practitioners, and other books are intended to provide the theoretical background and evidence for this practice. Energy medicine often shows that an imbalance in the body's "energy field" causes disease, and restoration of balance can restore the physique's liveliness arena to wellbeing. Some forms define healing by way of liberating the physique from undesirable energy or blocking the "heart." Diseases or episodes of the disease after treatment are called "ejection" or "contraction" in the mind. In general, doctors recommend additional treatment for complete treatment.

The "National Center for Complementary and Integrative Health (NCCIH)" distinguishes between medical services known as "true energy drugs" and medical methods called "energy" that is not physically detectable, including scientifically observable energy. You can check. He called it "Estimated Energy."

Forms of "veritable energy medicine" comprise light therapy, magnetic treatment, and color puncture. Medicinal technologies that practice electromagnetic emission (such as magnetic resonance imaging or radiation healing) stay not deliberated "energy products" in alternative medicine.

The type of "putative energy medicine" refers to therapeutic treatment using biological energy therapy, which states that the hand directs or regulates "energy" that is believed to affect the healing of the patient; Mental healing and mental healing, sensory therapy, sensory treatment, soft hand, esoteric healing, self-healing (the former term should not be confused with magnetic therapy), dental healing, Reiki, crystal healing, remote healing. Ideas for instance "Chi (Qi)," Prana," "congenital Intelligence," "Mana," "Pneuma," "Vital Fluid," "Odic Power" and "Orgone" are some of the expressions used to refer to this claimed energy field. This group does not apply to "acupuncture," Ayurvedic medicine, manual therapy, and more methods of manipulating the necessary energy with the help of physical manipulations.

The polar therapy, established by "Randolph Stone," is a form of energy source founded on the assumption that human wellbeing is exposed to affirmative and undesirable burdens of the electromagnetic field. The treatment of various human diseases, from muscle tension to cancer, has become popular. Though, conferring to "the American Cancer Society," existing scientific proof doesn't sustenance the claim that polar psychotherapy is operational in treating cancer or more diseases. "

Chapter 2 Types of Energy Healing

Here exist various diverse types of energy healing. These forms of healing cover a lot of types—more than 100 types are known.

Sound Healing Therapy

Acoustic therapy uses aspects of music to improve health, physical, and emotional well-being. The attending person participates in the experience with a trained speech specialist. Sound healing includes listening to music for music, translating music into the rhythms of music, changing the performance of instruments, and much more. There are several types of acoustics, including vibration therapy, which uses special sounds that create vibrational thoughts to increase brain waves.

It is believed that sound therapy began in ancient Greece when music was used to treat mental disorders. Historically, music was used to enhance the morale of the army, allowed people to work faster and more productively, and protected evil spirits with songs. Recent studies have linked music to a variety of health benefits, from improved immune function, reduced stress levels, and improved health in premature babies.

Types of Sound Therapy

There are several types of acoustic therapy, each of which has different effects, but not all have been proven.

Vibroacoustic Therapy

Vibrations are thought to affect body functions such as blood pressure and respiration. Acoustic vibration therapy uses sound vibrations to improve health and reduce stress. This type of acoustic therapy involves transferring music and sound directly to the body using the built-in speakers, mattresses, and special mats. There are several signs that show the ability to increase relaxation and relieve pain and symptoms in cancer patients and patients who recover from surgery.

Guided Meditation

Guided intervention is a kind of voice healing to meditate with voice guidance during a session, lesson, video, or application. Meditation may include invoking or invoking mantras or prayers. Studies show that meditation offers various health benefits, including reducing stress, anxiety, and depression, increasing memory, lowering blood pressure, reducing pain, lowering cholesterol and lowering the risk of heart disease and stroke.

Bonny Method

Bonnie's Way Helen L. Bonnie uses classical music and imagery to explore personal growth, awareness, and change. According to a 2017 study, there is promising evidence that a series of sessions can improve the mental and physiological health of adults with medical and mental needs.

Nordoff-Robbins

This sound restoration method is provided by a qualified musician who holds a two-year master's degree at Nordoff-Robbins. Use music that is familiar with the subject, create new music together, or perform. This approach is used to treat children with developmental disabilities and parents, mental health, learning disabilities and autism, dementia, and other disorders.

Singing Bowl Therapy

Klangbechertherapie was built in the 12th century and is used in Tibetan culture for meditation and rituals. The metal bowl creates a deep, clear sound, which is used to relax and restore the mind. A 2016 study shows that meditation in a bowl reduces stress, anger, depression, and fatigue. All this, as you know, affects physical health and increases the risk of illness.

Neurologic Music Therapy

Music therapy can reduce stress and increase relaxation. It has been proven that it is more effective than prescription drugs in reducing preoperative anxiety. A study published in 2017 found that a 30-minute session of music therapy relieves pain through traditional spinal surgery. Music therapy is performed by a provider who is authorized to assess human needs. This procedure includes making music, listening, singing, or moving. It is used to treat physical rehabilitation, pain, and brain damage.

Brainwave Entertainment

This method, also known as binaural beats, stimulates the brain under certain conditions. Pulsating tones are used to increase the level of rhythm and align brain waves. It helps improve focus, entry, rest, or sleep. Further research is needed, but there are some signs. A reliable source of brainwashing, which relieves anxiety, pain, and symptoms of premenstrual syndrome and enhances behavioral problems in children.

Turning Fork Therapy

In tuning fork therapy, calibrated metal forks are used to apply specific vibrations to various parts of the body. This can help reduce stress and energy and improve emotional balance. It works like acupuncture and uses sound frequencies for point stimulation rather than needles. There are several studies showing that fork therapy can relieve muscle and bone pain.

How Sound Healing Works

Voice control uses various aspects of sound to improve emotional and physical well-being. How it works depends on the acoustics used. Most wellness sessions are conducted independently by specially trained doctors. This session may include sitting or lying down, listening to music or sound from a speaker or instrument, or using special tools such as fork settings. Depending on the method, you may be silent, not singing, not moving, not using an instrument, and not moving to make a sound.

Benefits of Sound Healing

Good care is used to treat the symptoms of various disorders, such as depression, post-traumatic stress, anxiety disorder, autism, dementia, and behavioral disorders, as well as mental disorders with learning disabilities.

Instruments Used in Sound Healing

In addition to the sound, there are several instruments used to heal the sound: Cane-Forkspan drum flute song. This includes the use different instruments at once in many ways, including a guitar, piano or other instruments

Touch therapy

In some energy therapies, the user uses a soft touch or the patient's hands to send energy to the body or balance the energy of the body. Proponents say the benefits of this therapy come from increased vitality or balance. Others suggest that the benefits are due to survival factors such as: For example, the biological effects of contact and the psychological effects of experience with health.

Reiki

This is used as a form of alternative therapy—Reiki—which usually called energy therapy. It appeared in Japan at the end of the 19th century is also alleged to include the transmission of collective energy to a patient beginning at the hands of a specialist. Some arguments relate to Reiki since this one is difficult to verify its success scientifically. But a lot of individuals who get Reiki confess that it functions and is growing in reputation. A 2007 study found that 1.2 million adults in the United States attempted Reiki or related treatments at a minimum of once last year. It is estimated that over 60 hospitals provide Reiki services for patients.

About Reiki

The term "Reiki," meaning "mystical atmosphere, a magical sign." This originates after the Japanese words, "rei" (worldwide) plus "Ki" (life energy). Reiki exists as a kind of energy treatment. Healing energy is directed to the drive arenas nearby the physique. Conferring to specialists, physical trauma, or emotional pain can lead to stagnation of energy in the body. Over time, this energy blockage can bring about disease.

This energy treatment purposes of maintaining energy stream besides eliminating blockages like acupuncture or acupressure. Practitioners said that increasing the stream of liveliness throughout the physique may provide easing, ache relief, quick curing, and additional signs of the disease. Reiki has remained everywhere for many thousand years. This method was initially established in 1922 via Japanese Buddhism under the named Mikao Usui. This practice spread in the 1940s through Hawaii to the United States and further in the 1980s to Europe. This is usually called hand care, otherwise direct care.

Techniques Used in Reiki
Related technologies have the following names: Focus on scattering while pumping, rotating and tilting, extracting dangerous energy extraction. Aura Some Reiki practitioners use it when a healing crystal or chakra can provide healing or protection.

A session can go from fifteen to ninety minutes. The amount of periods depends on whatever the patient wants to do. Other patients choose one session, while others prefer a series of sessions to solve specific problems.

Happenings in Reiki Sessions

Reiki is great kept in comfortable conditions, but then again can happen in anyplace. The client sits in a relaxed seat, otherwise puts a full dress on the table. Depending on the preferences of the patient, there may or may not be music. Practitioners use different forms of hands for two to five minutes to gently place their hands on certain areas of the head, limbs, and chest. The arm may be placed on 20 diverse parts of the physique. If you have specific damage (for example—you can hold your hand directly above the wound when you are burned. Energy transfer occurs when the practitioner gently grabs your hand above or above your body. Keep respective arm locations till the specialist insinuates that liveliness no longer flows in. A practitioner can raise his hand and place it in another area of the body when he feels that the heat or energy in his hand is asleep.

Health Benefits

Practitioners say that the healing effect is mediated by the delivery of widespread liveliness, well-known as "qi."

In India, it is well-known as "Prana." This exists as liveliness associated with "tai chi" exercises. This exists as vital liveliness which other people trust atmospheres us completely. This liveliness must penetrate the physique. Reiki specialists note that liveliness is not measured using new technology, but many people who prepared it can feel it. It is believed that Reiki improves relaxation, supports the natural process of healing the body, supports emotive, intellectual, and mystical welfare. It's furthermore alleged that it provides profound easing, helps individuals overcome complications, release emotive tension, and progress general well-being. Those that take Reiki call this one "very convenient."

Situations which Reiki has existed to support treatment are:

Malignance Heart disease Nervousness Hopelessness

Prolonged ache Barrenness

Neurodegenerative ailments "Autism"

Crohn's illness Exhaustion disorders

Malignance patients that underwent Reiki said they felt improved later. This can be for the reason that it aids in ease. Additional cause, conferring to malignance study in the UK. Perhaps the therapist can spend a stint together and touch them. It possesses some calming effect on patients who may be affected by invasive treatment, anxiety, besides tension. People claim diverse experiences. Others said that practitioners' arms became hotter, some saw cold hands, and some experienced trembling waves. The most common report is stress reduction and deep relaxation.

Evidence of Reiki's Healing Power

As Reiki becomes popular, the answer remains. Reiki allows you to relax, relieve pain, heal quickly, and some symptoms, but some studies say that it supports certain health benefits. He was charged with claiming to have cured the disease without scientific evidence. Some describe his claim as a fraud. Critics say they fly earlier than our current understanding of natural law. Advocates say the profits of well-being besides tension reduction is actual, but they are difficult to a degree through systematic research. Researchers have found that there is no qualitative study of the effect. According to him, there are no studies showing that it's further operative than a "placebo."

Analysis of the literature available in 2008 showed there wasn't adequate proof in backing Reiki as an operative healing for the disease besides that its worth has not been proven. In 2015, a study was published on the treatment of Cochrane anxiety and depression. Researchers conclude that "there is not enough evidence that Reiki is suitable for people 16 years of age or older with anxiety, depression, or both." Utmost few researches performed were of meager value, small sample size, and without expert judgment or a control group. Studies published by BMC Nephrology, on the other hand, show that it may be beneficial to provide a "therapeutic effect" to patients on dialysis, especially if it is provided free of charge by a volunteer. Pain relief may be weak, but not traumatic and not dangerous, and the patient feels "working" to relieve pain.

"Annie Harrington" recently voiced to "MNT" that the "Reiki Federation of the United States" currently has a large document, "to facilitate a lot of research." These results, which are being studied by the Federal Council on Supplemental Health and Natural Health (CNHC), are likely to help bring Reiki to the mainstream.

Safety of Reiki

"The US National Center for Complementary and Integrated Health (NCCIH)" says Reiki "has not proven its health benefits." But no side effects appeared. The main health problem is that people with serious health problems can choose Reiki and other additional methods of treatment, rather than strictly testing modern medicines. But this cannot be combined with other dangerous treatments. In fact, touching the "universal energy," it seems to have several advantages: from building confidence to improving overall well-being. Kosovo suggests that the costly existing treatments available today frequently have graveside paraphernalia besides could or could not be effective. Therefore, several individuals want to freely choose an alternative.

Where to Get Reiki

Reiki is becoming increasingly popular. A sense of well-being and less danger of injury. Equally an outcome, Reiki is currently accessible in other large clinics. For example, other health care workers, including hospitals, could provide you uncharged services as a portion of calmative maintenance. Secluded Reiki sessions range as of 30$ to 100$ which usually doesn't have a cover. Anybody looking for a trained and skilled Reiki specialist ought to pay attention to this because there are very few rules in this area. It will be helpful to ask practitioners about his education, together with professionalism. Reiki isn't a substitute medicine for curative problems, nonetheless an additional medicine that helps to heal and improve your health. It is best to consult with alternative doctors first.

How to be a Reiki Practitioner and Regulations

No teaching, tutoring, or practice is required to participate in Reiki preparation or tablets. In this method called "strong spiritual experience," the teacher delivers liveliness and curing to the scholar. Reiki teaching is different; a lot of students will study on energy throughout the physique, working with energy healing, and working with clients. To prepare for strengthening, you need to fast for two to three days, meditate, concentrate on the environment, and cause undesirable reactions. There exist three championship stages. Individuals who have reached the chief stage can learn from other individuals and receive distance treatment in the form of degrees.

Regulators at times request Reiki sites to transform their facts in accordance with authorized ethics. Locations vending Reiki merchandise could be held liable by maintaining that such a product is not a medicinal means and shouldn't be used to diagnose, treat, cure, or prevent any disease. The British Advertising Standards Organization (ASA) rejected the claim that Reiki can cure several diseases in many cases. Judy Kosovich presented a "new perspective" on the regulation of energy medicine in a study published by Physics Practical. Recognizing that there are governing forms to guard the community, he claims that additional action is needed as a means that is not understood or explained by scientific research.

Therapeutical Touch

Therapeutic Touch (usually abbreviated as "TT"), well-known as "Non- Contact Therapeutic Touch (NCTT)," is a "pseudoscientific" liveliness healing that helps physicians promote soothing, reduce ache together with unease. "Touch Therapy" is a listed symbol in Canada aimed at "practical and homogenous treatment practices executed by specialists who are sensitive to the area of liveliness received around the body. No contact required." Sensory physicians show that the patient's energy field can be recognized and manipulated by placing the patient's hand next to or near the patient. According to a broadly named research printed by the "Journal of the American Medical Association" in 1998, when Emily Rose was nine years old, sensory doctors could identify the existence of an arm a little edges overhead revelation. She stayed disconnected. "Simon Singh and Edward Ernst," inside their manuscript "Trick or Treat," concluded that "the field of energy is just an invention of a healing imagination." The "American Cancer Society" identified that "the available scientific evidence does not support the claim that TT can treat cancer or other diseases." The 2014 Cochrane Report established no convincing proof to support wound healing.

Dora Kunz, a theologian and former chairman of the Theosophical Society of America (1975-1987) and "Dolores Krieger," now a lecturer of nursing at "New York University," established healing contacts during 1970. According to Krieger, sensory therapy is not associated with religion or healing beliefs but is based on ancient healing practices, such as ordination. "A doctor (client) is the one who ultimately heals himself, so the doctor or therapist acts as a system for supporting human energy until the therapeutic immune system itself is sufficiently absorbed," Krieger said.

The validity of TT is carried out in the field of the science of modern man, associated with the mystical interpretation of Martha E. Rogers and quantum mechanics, especially the last of Fritiof Capra. The 2002 review did not find any of the two reasons to refute. Rogers 'theory turned out to be incompatible with the principles of TT, and the duplicate term was caused by a lack of accuracy in Rogers' work, which was very important for him. The reason for the interpretation of physics is that the "global interconnection" of the universe allows for remote healing. Followers of TT will be involved in interpreting "Bell's theory," together with the likelihood of substantial dysfunction. The understanding isn't reinforced with investigational data.

A 2002 research resolved that "TT theory is inexplicable" and that "evidence supporting the current situation with physical energy should be considered as evidence for TT theory." A procedure named "electron resonance transfer," that "physicist Alan Sokal" calls "nonsense."

Researched Evidence

During the years, numerous researches have been conducted to verify the effectiveness of TT, and one or more systematic reviews have been conducted with various meta-analyzes and various outcomes then deductions. "O'Matuna et al." When deliberating this researches, highlight issues that include the tendency to publish additional medical journals that cannot rule out the wrong research methodology and "outperform studies with positive results." They approve that taking in consideration contextual methodical information, the predecessor acceptability of TT is adequately low that any procedural mistake in research could constantly offer a further conceivable account for some optimistic discoveries.

"— O'Mathúna et al."

"Emily Rose," a nine-year-old, developed as well as conducted research of sensory therapy. Using the assistance of "Stephen Barrett of Quack watch and RN's mother Linda Rose," Emily became the youngest naturopath research group to take documents from the American Medical Association (JAMA) and participate in therapeutic touch research. Twenty-one therapists participated in the study and tried to find their aura. Specialists set up right across the wooden umbrella, and Emily set upright at the other end. Then the specialists put their arms in the hovels on the wood. Emily threw a coinage, helping to decide the hand the doctor would close (of course, without touching). Then, practitioners should indicate whether they can sense the biofield and where their hands are. All participants stated that they could do it, but the real consequences do not confirm the requirements they needed. Conducting recurring attempts, specialists can find their hands at a level that is not significantly different from a match. JAMA Editor George D. Lundberg, MD, advises casualties together with cover corporations to refrain from waging for healing, or first ask if the payment is accepted or not until an honest experiment works.

There isn't existing medicinal proof for the efficiency of sensory therapy. "Cochrane's systematic review of this is not conclusive evidence that TT contributes to acute wound healing, and the American Cancer Society does not support claims that TT can cure cancer or other diseases."

How TT Works

Researchers remain not sure in what way sensory therapy helps, although there are two notions. The first notion suggests that the patient's cells have pain associated with painful physical or emotional experiences, such as infections, injuries, or complex relationships. The ache kept in those cells is destructive, thus stops other cells from functioning well with some cells in the physique. Thus leads to illness. Specialists trust that tonic contact improves wellbeing by reinstating intercellular communiqué. Another notion is grounded on the principle of substantial physical science. When iron lifeblood flows in the body, an electromagnetic arena is created. Conferring to the notion, we can altogether effortlessly recognize the area named the "aura," but currently simply definite individuals, for example, those with calming contacts, get this capability.

In general, the relaxing effect is founded on the impression that well-being needs a sensible stream of living loveliness. Therapists feel the energy with their own hands and send healthy energy. In treatment, ordinary people experience warmness, easing, and ache liberation. A specialist says that your liveliness is burning or icy, energetic or inactive, clogged or loose. There exist eight main areas where the energy of the physique, head, neck, heart, abdomen, lower abdomen, sacral, knees, and feet are felt. But a person who receives therapeutic contact is a doctor. A doctor provokes only the healing mechanisms of the body itself. The role of practitioners is to support this process.

Happenings in TT Session

Before starting the session, the therapist asks you to sit down or lie down. You do not need to take off your clothes. A session can be divided into four stages: the center. The therapist "centers" using breathing, visualization and meditation to achieve a change in the state of consciousness about himself

Assessment

The therapist holds two to four edges as of the physique when touching commencing at the head to the toes. The purpose of doing this is to estimate the liveliness arena around the body. Counselors regularly define heat, cold, congestion, and tingling in an "overloaded" or "blocked" energy field.

Intervention

When the therapist discovers a blockage or blockage, he moves his hands in rhythm, starting from the top of the blockade and dropping from the body. This action, called fragmentation, is recurrent until the specialist does not feel constipated or at ease. The therapist also visualizes and transfers vital liveliness to precise parts of the physique to precise imbalance.

Assessment/conclusion

After a few minutes of rest, you ask the therapist the feeling you are having. The specialist can recheck the liveliness arena to see if there are blockages.

Health Benefits of TT

Most studies show that sensory therapy can relieve tension headaches and relieve pain. Blisters, osteoarthritis, or pain after surgical procedure. It could as well accelerate injury curing besides advance purpose in patients with inflammation of the legs. As a matter of fact, research indicates that healing contact arouses cell development. The healing touch similarly enhances easing. Patients with heart disease, cancer, besides burns report that therapeutic contact significantly reduces anxiety. As a rule, unfathomable easing linked to healing contact lessens tension, depresses blood stress, and recovers inhalation. Relaxation can likewise lessen fat and progress immunity and lower abdomen function. Only one treatment can reduce the difficulty of pregnancy.

Therapeutic contact may be useful in many other conditions besides treatment, including:

Fibromyalgia Slumber apnea

Fidgety limb disorder, an ailment that sources sleeplessness Antipathies

Bronchitis

Dependences

Lupus

Alzheimer's ailment, probably, some methods of dementia Prolonged ache

Other individuals said they felt emotive and mystical alterations when getting a healing contact. Such as better confidence, self-control, and self- esteem. The question of whether the healing power of touch is connected with "on-hand" remains a moot point. Critics argue that the healing observed after a therapeutic touch is associated with relaxation features that come with the treatment, besides the transmission of energy amid the specialist's arms together with the human physique.

Safety of TT

You can safely use sensory therapy as part of your care. There are no studies are showing that therapeutic contact is effective in all types of diseases. However, some health experts believe this can help with stress and anxiety. Those who come for treatment say that they have a fresh heart; they heal faster and feel better. Talk with your doctor about attempts or other additional medical practices that you already use. If your doctor knows all your medical recommendations, they will help you manage your health.

How to Become a TT Practitioner

Sensory therapy skills are taught not only in health contact schools but also in colleges, medical schools, nursing programs, and massage schools. During the session, the client fully dresses on the massage table. Doctors then use soft or physical contact (not in direct contact) to manipulate and balance the client's energy field, often feeling deep relaxation and calm. A session usually takes 40-60 minutes. Therapeutic sensory massage is used to treat stress and pain, recover from surgery, treat cancer, and treat other acute and chronic diseases.

Sensory healing programs are generally intended for practitioners in specific areas, such as healthcare or physical activity. At Touch Healing School, you will learn the relationship between the body's energy system and health, as well as special skills for treating touch. More advanced courses focus on work ethics and practice. Some programs may include instructions for related forms, such as Reiki Healing Touch. Certification for Therapeutic Sensory Therapy is provided by specialized organizations such as the Touch Treatment Program, a training program accredited as the Touch Therapy Practitioner (HTP). Healing across Borders, a non-profit organization that provides Touch Healing Practitioner (CHTP) certified certification. These two accreditation programs have been approved by the American Association of Holistic Nurses and the National Certification Council for Massage and Body Therapy.

ETF

EFT is a form of modern, rapidly developing expansion together individual healing which has been a technique used for a wide range of issues in the arena of liveliness psychology. Getting the roots from psychology, acupuncture, and kinesiology. It exists as an extremely operational and tender way to adapt to the sensation you want to change, to the energy system of your body. EFT is used to improve and develop people. Develop attitude and behavior, solve individual complications, fears, and reduce stress. EFT is very operational once it is used in all kinds of top metrics (e.g., sporting, civic talking, transactions, performing, etc.)

With EFT, certain "acupressure" parts of the physique are touched using tips of the fingers, while the problem is central. The procedure could be recurrent to reduce the force until the equilibrium is reinstated. This all happens normally in a chair. With the right EFT implementation, more than 80 percent of customers achieve a real improvement or complete problem- solving. Sessions can be held directly on the phone or Skype; all you have to do is get in contact with a specialist.

Advantages of ETF

He often works elsewhere. Usually, it is fast, durable, and soft and easy to learn. You can install it yourself. There are no side effects. There is no surgical intervention. Without pushing or stretching the body, there is no equipment, needles, pills, or chemicals.

Significant improvement or complete cure in many case studies; Undesirable Feelings

Diet Desires

Decreasing or Removing Ache, Ache Controlling

Cig Dependence and Drug dependence, Liquor misuse Aversions and Fears

Unease and Terror Spasms Forces and Preoccupations

Misery and Sorrow, Anguish and Forfeiture

Guiltiness and Mistrustfulness, Fury and Fright Sleeplessness and Bad dream

Undesirable Recollections

PTSD and Disturbing Commemorations Erotic Mishandling Concerns

Self-perception and Coyness Dyslexia

Top Presentation

enhancing Attentiveness and Concentration Fulfilling Affirmative Objectives

Civic Communication

doing Examinations and Interviews

Acupuncture

"Acupuncture" is a method of substitute medication and the main constituent of "traditional Chinese medicine (TCM)," where skinny prickles are introduced to the physique. Acupuncture is "pseudoscience," for the reason that the theory, together with the practice of TCM, is not based scientifically and are called shamans. There are various acupuncture options that have arisen from different philosophies, and the technology depends on the country in which they are performed. It is recommended by acupuncture for various other disorders but is most often used to relieve ache. It is commonly used in amalgamation with additional methods of healing.

Various acupuncture studies and systematic reviews do not match, indicating a lack of effect. A Cochrane review found that acupuncture is ineffective under various conditions. Systematic reviews by doctors in the "University of Exeter and Plymouth" have revealed slight proof of the effects of acupuncture on pain. Overall, data show that short-term acupuncture treatments do not have lasting aids. Other studies have shown that acupuncture can relieve some form of ache, but most studies have shown that the effects of acupuncture may not be brought about by the healing itself. An organized assessment showed that the palliative result brought by acupuncture seems to have no medical significance, which is indistinguishable from distortion. An analysis shows that acupuncture for prolonged lower vertebral ache is economical in addition to ordinary treatments, and a detached organized assessment does not provide sufficient evidence of the cost-effectiveness of acupuncture for treating chronic lower vertebral ache.

Acupuncture is mostly harmless if trained by a skilled user by means of hygienic needles and a disposable needle. With proper delivery, the percentage of the smallest side effects is small. However, there are accidents and infections associated with neglect of a doctor, especially when using sterilization methods. A 2013 survey shows that the intelligence of conduction has improved considerably over the past period. The utmost common side effects are pneumothorax and infection. As serious side effects continue to be reported, appropriate training is recommended to minimize the danger for acupuncturists.

Systematic studies haven't been able to find any physiological or histological proof found in customary Chinese conceptions which include "qi, meridians and acupuncture points," and numerous current practices do not have the main component of the early belief system: vital energy (qi) or meridian. It does not support existence. Acupuncture is supposed to be about "100 BC." China was created when classic medicine of Emperor Yuangdi Neking was published, but some experts suspect that this drug was indeed used in advance. As time went by, contradictory statements and faith methods concerning the influence of the circulation of the moon, sky, earth, yin and yang and the "rhythm" of the body appeared in the effectiveness of treatment. The popularity of acupuncture in China has ceased owing to modifications in national civil governance together with the preferences of western medication or rationalism. In the 6th century, AD acupuncture first extended to Korea, through to Japan via health campaigners and from France then to Europe. When spreading to the western countries together with the United States in the 20th century, mystical components of acupuncture, contrary to Western notions, were sometimes left to simply attach acupuncture points.

Clinical Research

Acupuncture is an alternative treatment. It is also used to treat various symptoms but is most often used to relieve ache. Acupuncture is commonly cast-off in amalgamation with some procedures of cure. For instance, the "American Society of Anesthesiologists" claims that healing for non- inflammatory and non-specific lower vertebral ache can solely be considered in combination with existing treatments.

In acupuncture, needles are inserted in the skin. Conferring to the "Medical Education and Research

Foundation (Mayo Clinic)," the general period is interrupted when 5 to 20 needles are inserted. In most circumstances, the needle can remain in position for ten to twenty minutes. This may be due to the use of high temperature, stress, or laser radiation. In general, it is grounded in intuition and philosophy, not even an individual and systematic study. In Japan, there exists a non-invasive treatment established during the early years of the 20th century by the use of a series of complex prickles to treat children (Shonychin or Shawnee Hari).

Clinical practice varies from country to country. Evaluation of the regular amount of clients cured each hour shows substantial variances amongst the United States (1.2) and China (10). Chinese herbal medicine is regularly in use. There are different approaches to acupuncture that relate to different philosophies. Various acupuncture practices have developed, but methods that are cast-off in "traditional Chinese medicine (TCM)" are the utmost common in the United States. Customary acupuncture includes a syringe, cauterization, and cup healing, which could be complemented by some techniques, which include heart rate together with some physique and language recognition tests. Customary acupuncture suggests that "qi" flows throughout the physique along the meridian. The key techniques that the UK uses are BMT together with Western healing acupuncture. The word "Western Medical Acupuncture" refers to the alteration of acupuncture grounded on BMT with a smaller amount of emphasis on BMT. "Western medical acupuncture" approaches include the use of acupuncture after a medical diagnosis. A normal for limited acupuncture points do not exist since the contrasting acupuncture systems used in different countries are compared to identify different acupuncture points.

In traditional acupuncture, acupuncturists determine the treatment that should be treated by observing and asking patients in accordance with tradition. TCM uses four diagnostic methods: examination, stethoscope, and odor, examination, and palpation. On examination, much focus is given to the facade and especially the patois, such as examination of the tension, color, shape, size, and range of the tongue, as well as the presence of plaque around the edges. Auscultation and smell include listening to certain noises, which include wheeziness, and attention to physique scent. The study focused on the "seven surveys": colds and illness; Sweating Hungriness, dehydration and palate; Excretion and urine; Ache; Slumber; menstruation, and a white stream. Soft press focuses on the sensation of the physique of thin points "a-shea" and sensations of the pounding.

Needles

The utmost communal method for stimulating acupuncture is the use of penetration into the skin through skinny metallic prickles, that are controlled by hand, or using electrically stimulated devices (electroacupuncture), the needle can be further stimulated. Acupuncture prickles are usually prepared by "stainless steel," which is malleable and prevents rust or damage. Prickles are frequently thrown away afterward to avoid infection. Recyclable prickles must be sanitized after using them on a patient. The length of the needle is 13 to 130 mm (0.51 to 5.12 inches), with short prickles close to the facade together with the eyes and long prickles in thick matters. The diameter of the needle is from 0.16 to 0.46 mm. Thick needles are used for healthy patients. Thin needles can be flexible and require the insertion of a tube. Although blunt needles cause more pain, the top of the prickle must not be very piercing to avert damage.

In addition to thread-shaped needles, other types of needles comprise three- blade prickles and nine old prickles. Japanese acupuncture specialists consider very skinny prickles on the surface; other times, it does not penetrate the skin and is surrounded by well-known tubes(17th-century inventions adopted in the west and china). Acupuncture in Korea's copper needles are used and focuses more on weapons.

Needle Techniques Insertion

Sterilization is done on the skin, and the needle is injected into the flexible directing pipe. The needle can be handled in many methods, such as rotating, blinking, or moving the skin up and down. Most of the ache is sensed in the epidermal layer of the membrane, so it is better to place the needle quickly. Often the needle is stimulated by the hand, causing a gray, confined, painful feeling known as "De Qi," and the tingling experienced by the specialist, and the perfunctory relations amid the prickle and membrane. Sore Acupuncture techniques can affect pain, and an experienced doctor can use the needle minus producing ache.

De-qi

"De-qi" "(Chinese: 得气 ; pinyin: dé qì; "arrival of qi")." De-qi indicates tingling, swelling, or electric tingling, which is transmitted to the needle position. If this sensation is not observed, inaccurate sharp positions, incorrect depth of penetration of the needle, incorrect physical handling is to blame. If "De-Qi" isn't observed instantly during the injection of the needle, several physical influence methods are frequently used to facilitate the insertion of the needle (e.g., "pooling," "shaking" or "shaking").

After observing the solution, the technique can be used to "influence" the solution. For example, they say that a certain lethal dish is repelled from the body by means of certain manipulations. Other technologies are aimed at "improvement" "(Chinese: 补 ; pinyin: bǔ)" or "sedating" "(Chinese: 泄 ; pinyin: xiè) qi." The first method is used for the deficit model and the second for the increase model. De Qi is extra essential for Chinese acupuncture, but Japanese and western patients cannot be considered an important part of treatment.

Related Searches

Acupuncture is often accompanied by swelling, burns of moxa (dry moss) on or close to the membrane, but frequently not close or not at the acupuncture part. Acupuncture is traditional treatment for acute illnesses, and cauterization is used for chronic diseases. Cauterization can be applied directly to the skin of cauterization, either directly (a cone can be applied directly to the skin and burn the skin with the formation of blisters and scars), or indirect (or cauterization of garlic, ginger or chopped vegetables or cylinders).

Cupping is an ancient Chinese alternative medicine that causes topical inhalation of the skin. Practitioners believe that this mobilizes a cycle to endorse curing.

"Tui na" is a "TCM" method that uses many empty-handed techniques in which needles are not used to stimulate qi flow.

Electro-acupuncture is a method of acupuncture in that acupuncture prickles are put into a ruse that causes a constant electric shock (the so-called "stimulation of a transdermal electric nerve mask called acupuncture [TENS]").

"Fire needle acupuncture," also called fire aggravating, is a procedure for swiftly placing a hot prickle on parts of the physique.

Menopause is an incentive for the physique, such as acupuncture, which uses sound instead of needles. This can be done using a sensor that directs narrow ultrasonic light from 6-8 centimeters to the acupuncture point of the meridian in the body. Alternatively, you can use a tuning fork or other sound output devices.

Acupuncture injections are injections of various substances (e.g., medicines, herbal extracts or vitamins) to acupuncture. This method associates old-fashioned acupuncture with effective doses of injections of frequently approved drugs, making an argument that it can be additionally operative than a particular cure, specifically for treating several types of chronic pain. However, according to a review in 2016, most of the tests published for this technology are of little value due to methodological problems and will require more extensive tests to draw useful conclusions.

Ear artery therapy, identified as ear acupuncture, or acupuncture of the ear, is thought to have originated in earliest China. A needle is placed to stimulate the point of the external ear. A current method is established in France in the initial 1950s. Systematic proof that it could treat the disease is not available. There is little proof of helpfulness.

The acupuncture of the scalp established in Japan is grounded on reflex logical contemplations that belong to the scalp.

"Korean hand acupuncture" focuses on reflex zones. Medical acupuncture is trying to incorporate reflexology concepts, initiating part patterns, together with concepts of anatomy (which include the spreading of skin diseases) to acupuncture, emphasizing an extra formal method to localizing acupuncture points.

"Cosmetic acupuncture" This is using acupuncture to lessen facial creases.

Animal acupuncture is using acupuncture in pets. As for veterinary drugs, there is no detailed data on additional or alternative technologies, but the data is growing.

Efficiency

Acupuncture has been extensively studied. In 2013, about 1,500 randomized controlled acupuncture trials called PubMed were conducted. But the results of reviews of acupuncture effects are not decisive.

The development of rigorous research on acupuncture is complex, but not impossible. Acupuncture Due to the nature of acupuncture, the top main problems in efficiency studies is the development of a suitable placebo regulator. A research was made if acupuncture has a particular effect on the patient, the doctor, and blind analysis appear to be the most appropriate approach for "ruthless" forms of acupuncture. Artificial acupuncture uses needles or non-invasive needles at points other than acupuncture, for example, place the needle in a meridian that is not associated with the test condition, or in a position that is not connected with the meridian. This may be due to a completely unspecified effect or may indicate that improper treatment is not inactive or that a systematic protocol provides inadequate treatment.

According to a 2014 Nature Reviews Cancer report: "Unlike mechanisms that presumably divert the flow of qi through the meridian, researchers generally believe that the place where the needle is inserted as often as possible does not matter. (That is, there is no sleep-effect effect.) Even though the prickle is injected, that is, "acupuncture," "placebo," or "placebo" as a rule, has a similar effect as the "real" acupuncture, in other better circumstances acupuncture is effective for pain: the position in which the needle is placed, the amount of prickles in use, the user's familiarity or skill or condition during session (compared to false). The same analysis showed that the amount of prickles and periods is paramount. This is the result of an improvement in saliva compared to the control group without saliva due to the large number. There are several systematic studies in which the constituents of an acupuncture period could be vital for the healing consequence, comprising the location and deepness of saliva, the form, and strength of the stimulus, and the amount of prickles used. Studies show that needles should not stimulate or penetrate marked traditional acupuncture points to achieve the expected effect (e.g., psychosocial factors).

The "shy" acupuncture reaction to osteoarthritis can be used in older people, but placebo is generally considered fraud and therefore unethical. However, some doctors and ethics experts may suggest a placebo use state, which can be a hypothetical benefit of cheap cure minus side effects or drug or some drug interactions. Proof for utmost substitute medications, which include acupuncture, which is distant from convincing, so using substitute medication in conventional well-being can be a moral issue.

The application of proof-based medical principles to acupuncture study is still debatable having various implications. Some studies have shown that acupuncture can relieve pain, but most studies have shown that the effects of acupuncture are mainly caused by placebo. There is evidence that the profit of acupuncture is old. There is inadequate proof for the usage of acupuncture likened to mass therapy. Acupuncture isn't superior to a long basic cure. The usage of acupuncture has remained disapproved for the lack of scientific evidence about the effect or clear mechanism for its effectiveness in diseases other than placebo. Acupuncture is known as "Placebo Theater," and "David Gorsky" claims that while acupuncture advocates seek a "placebo effect" or develop a "meaningful placebo," they basically admit that it is more than just a drug.

Publication Bias

Publication bias was mentioned in a review of randomized control acupuncture studies (RCTs). An acupuncture study conducted in 1998 showed that tests from Japan, Hong Kong, Taiwan, and China were as useful as acupuncture, up to 10 out of 11 studies conducted in Russia. TCM quality assessment, including acupuncture in 2011, TCM resolved that the operational worth of utmost of these studies (such as methodology, investigational monitoring, and blindness) was normally low, especially in studies printed in the Chinese periodical. (I know that the worth of acupuncture tests is better than TCM testing tools). The study also showed that the quality of tests published in non-Chinese journals was higher. Chinese writers use more Chinese research, which turned out to be equally positive. According to an 88 systematic acupuncture trials review published in 2012, in Chinese periodicals, half or more of these appraisals stated prejudice tests, and most of them were printed in periodicals that had no effect. A study conducted in 2015, which compared records of previously registered acupuncture studies with published results, showed that participation in the study before the test was not uncommon. The study also showed that reports on sampled results and measurements modified to produce statistically significant results are often found in these writings.

Researcher and press officer "Steven Salzberg" usually refers to acupuncture and eastern medication as "fake medical journals," including meridian research and acupuncture in acupuncture and medicine.

Specific Conditions

Pain

Many studies and many systematic acupuncture tests are often inadequate. A systematic review of a 2011 systematic review showed that true acupuncture is not better than false acupuncture to treat pain, and some tests have concluded that acupuncture does not provide conclusive proof that this is an operational ache reliever. An identical study instituted that collar ache is one of 4 kinds of ache that are known to have a positive effect, but the main study used warned that there was a risk of serious displacement. A 2009 Cochrane review found that acupuncture is not effective for various conditions.

According to a systematic review conducted in 2014, the effectiveness of nocebo acupuncture is clinically significant and shows the extent to which side effects could make a measure of the "nocebo effect." "A meta-analysis" by the Collaboration of Acupuncture Trials in 2012 shows that "compared to herbal remedies" in treating four kinds of prolonged ache (urination and collar ache, lap arthritis, prolonged headache) and backache. I found a relatively simple acupuncture effectiveness. We settled for the fact that it was "more than a placebo" aside from being a sensible choice for the goal. Edward Ernst and David Kolhun mentioned a meta-analysis of minor clinical relevance. "I'm worried that I was able to get rid of this distortion," says Edward Ernst. The same researchers teamed up in 2017 to update its prior meta-analysis and once more established that acupuncture for certain musculoskeletal pains, arthritis, chronic pain in the head and shoulders is better than fake acupuncture. In addition, after a year, the effect of acupuncture decreased by about 15%.

According to a systematic review conducted in 2010, acupuncture is considered other than a "placebo-widespread" prolonged ache condition. However, the writers acknowledge it's not yet known whether the overall benefits are clinically significant or cost-effective. According to a review in 2010, real acupuncture and fake acupuncture have brought related progress which could be used only as proof of the effectiveness of acupuncture. A similar appraisal shows inadequate proof that actual and fake acupuncture yields biotic variances in spite of the same properties. A methodical appraisal and meta-analysis in 2009 showed acupuncture has a low palliative result, has no clinical significance, and is indistinguishable from prejudice. In the same study, it was not clear whether acupuncture eliminates pain, regardless of the psychological effects of conscious syringes. A 2017 methodical appraisal and meta-analysis showed that acupuncture of the ear could help reduce ache in a span of 48 hours after using; otherwise, the average variance concerning control and acupuncture was low.

Lower Back Pain

Acupuncture can be operative for non-specific subordinate backache, according to a 2013 appraisal. However, the writers pointed out that this study has the following limitations: In many studies, the heterogeneity of research characteristics and the low quality of the methodology. A 2012 methodical appraisal provided proof that acupuncture is further operative than the absence of non-specific chronic back pain. The evidence is contradictory and compared with other treatments. According to a systematic review of a 2011 systematic study, "For chronic lower back pain, personalized acupuncture is a toothpick that does not penetrate the skin and does not improve the symptoms of fake acupuncture or acupuncture." According to a 2010 review, champagne acupuncture was just as effective in treating chronic back pain as true acupuncture. Although the specific therapeutic effect of acupuncture is low, its benefits are clinically significant, mainly due to circumstances and psychosocial situations. Studies of brain tomography show that traditional and artificial acupuncture have different effects on the limbic system and have a similar analgesic effect. A Cochrane study in 2005 showed that for acute pain in the lower back, there was insufficient evidence of acupuncture or dry needles. The same study shows faint signs of pain relief and improvement in the short term immediately after treatment compared to lack of treatment or lower back pain. In a similar appraisal, we established that acupuncture is no longer operative than conservative and some substitute cures. According to a methodological appraisal and meta-analysis in 2017, collar ache can be compared to conventional acupuncture, while electro acupuncture reduces pain more effectively than regular acupuncture. The same review notes that "the included studies are difficult to complete because of the high risk of bias and inaccuracies." In the year 2015, a review of organized studies of various vaginas indicated that acupuncture could help patients with a chronic lower vertebral ache for a petite period. The appraisal showed this to be true when acupuncture is isolated or used in addition to existing treatments. A systematic review of the Clinical Practice Guide of the American College of Physicians for 2017 showed that there was slight proof of acupuncture being operative for chronic lower backache, or limited data on acute lower back pain. Strong evidence of two conditions in the same review. Back in 2017, clinical practice guidelines published by Danish health authorities recently recommended acupuncture for low back and lower back pain.

Headaches and Migraine

Two reviews of cocaine in 2016 showed that acupuncture could help prevent tension headaches and episodes of migraine. The 2016 Cochrane Acupuncture Assessment Study for Preventing Temporary Migraines concluded that true acupuncture has little effect on shamanic acupuncture. According to a 2012 review, acupuncture can help treat headaches, but safety needs to be documented in more detail to provide compelling recommendations in support of its use.

Some more uses included:

Elevated and truncated blood stress

Chemotherapy-influenced sickness and spewing Other digestive illnesses, comprising peptic sore

Hurting periods Dysentery

Hypersensitive rhinitis Faceache

Dawn illness

Rheumatoid inflammation Restoration

Element, tobacco and liquor reliance Backbone ache Strains

Tennis shove Lumbago Toothache

Decreasing the threat of stroke Prompting labor

Other situations are as follows: Fibromyalgia

Neuralgia Post-operative

Tourette pattern Rigid collar

Vascular dementia

Hooting cough, or pertussis

Benefits of Acupuncture

Acupuncture can help. However, there could be a few lateral properties. It could be efficiently shared with some cures. This could regulate several kinds of ache. Painkillers can aid the sick who are not suitable. NCCIH recommends that acupuncture never visit an existing doctor.

Expectations in Session

According to the theory of traditional Chinese medicine, acupuncture parts are situated on the meridian, where vibrant liveliness flows. This liveliness is called "qi" or qi. A specialist examines a client, assesses the patient's condition, uses one or even more than one thin, antiseptic prickles, and provides guidance on personal maintenance and some additional treatment methods, which include: B. Chinese herbal medicine. The client should lie on his back, front, or side, depending on the location of the needle. Acupuncturists should use sterile disposable needles. The insertion of each needle can cause the patient a very short tingling or numbness. After insertion of the needle, a feeling of dullness sometimes appears on the underside of the needle and disappears. Acupuncture is normally fairly aching less. Other times, after insertion, needles heats up or is electrically roused. The needle lasts from five to thirty minutes.

The amount of treatment required depends solely on the person. An individual with a prolonged disease could be needing treatment one to two times a week for several months. Acute problems usually improve after eight to twelve meetings.

Risks

Nearly all treatments come with threats and advantages.

Potential Acupuncture Threats: This is harmful if the patient has abnormal blood clotting or is taking blood solvents. Blood loss, hurting, and tenderness could happen at the placement. Non-sterilized prickles can contaminate a client. In very intermittent circumstances, the prickle can damage and ruin inner organs. There is a risk of lung collapse in the chest or back. This though happens rarely. "The U.S. Food and Drug Administration" regulates acupuncture prickles as therapeutic expedients. Production and labeling require some principles to be met. The prickles are disinfected, non-toxic and should only be labeled for single use by a certified physician. Same as corresponding treatments, it's recommended that you use them with existing treatments for chronic or serious illnesses.

How to Find a Practitioner

To find a licensed physician, visit the National Council for Acupuncture and Herbal Certification (NCCAOM). In most states, this agency requires a license from practitioners. Individuals are encouraged to enquire from specialists concerning their practice and education. "NCCIH" points out that other cover plans currently cater to acupuncture, but first, it's prudent to inquire if expenses are covered.

The cost is from 75 to 95 dollars and a regular visit from 50 to 70 dollars.

Crystal Healing

Crystal treatment is a substitute medical procedure that uses semiprecious "crystals" such as quartz, amethyst, or opal. Proponents of the technology claim that there is no scientific basis for this statement, but it has healing power. On the one hand, the practitioner makes decisions in other parts of the body, often in the chakras. On the contrary, the practitioner makes decisions all over the body to build an energy network that surrounds clients with healing energy. However, studies show that the assertion that chakras or energy tissues do exist has not been confirmed, and there is no evidence that crystalline therapy has a bigger consequence on the physique than supplementary placebo. For this reason, it's deliberated pseudoscience.

Gemstones are considered an object that can help to heal in various cultures. Arizona Hopi Native Americans use quartz crystals for fortune- telling, which also localizes pain or causes illness in the body. Hopi traditionally uses crystals for other types of fortune-tellers, such as prisms, for crystals that direct sunlight to medical pallets, as well as for other forms of consciousness, such as controlling the strength and intensity of crystals. Gemstones are considered an object that can help to heal in various cultures. Arizona Hopi Native Americans use quartz crystals for fortune- telling, which also localizes pain or causes illness in the body. Hopi traditionally uses crystals for other types of fortune-tellers, such as prisms, for crystals that direct sunlight to medical pallets, as well as for other forms of consciousness, such as controlling the strength and intensity of crystals.

In the English-speaking world, crystal healing is associated with new conscious ritual movements, such as the "bourgeois healing activity of the New Era of Perfection." Unlike other forms of complementary and alternative medicine (CAM), participants in crystal therapy see this practice as "individual." I. H. depends on extreme personalization and creative expression. When you start the healing crystal, certain physical characteristics, such as shape, color, and marking, determine the location that can be treated with stones. The list of links is published in plain text. Ironically, practitioners claim that "the solution has no essential characteristics, but the quality is different between the two participants."

After choosing stones in accordance with their color or metaphysical characteristics, they are placed on the body.

Scientific Evidence

There is no scientific evidence that decision processing works. This is considered fake science. The success of decision processing is due to the placebo effect. In addition, there is no scientific basis for "blocking" the concept of "chakra," that is, the energy network or a similar term that needs to be justified. It is well known that these are just terms that followers use to convey their practice. The methodical word, energy, is a precise, clearly explained notion that can be easily measured and resembles the concept of esoteric energy used by proponents of fertilization therapy.

Williams, a French researcher, shepherded research to examine the strength of crystals comparing it to placebo in 1999. Eighty unpaid workers were requested to deliberate on placebo or quartz stones, which are vague from quartz. Numerous partakers said that they felt a characteristic "crystal effect." But whether this decision is genuine or placebo. In 2001, Christopher French, director of the "Department of Anomalistic Psychology Research at the University of London" and a member of Goldsmiths College, discussed a crucial study that went beyond the placebo effect at the annual meeting of the British Psychological Association. "

The healing effect of the decision can also be associated with cognitive distortions (what happens when a believer really wants to practice and sees only those who support this desire). Other veterinary institutions, including the "British Veterinary Association," warn that this method has not been methodically confirmed and that individuals ought to look for veterinary guidance beforehand in exhausting substitute methods, but fertilization treatments are also used on animals.

Qigong

Qigong (/ˈtʃiːɡɒŋ/), [1] "qi gong," "chi Kung," or "chi gung" (shortened Chinese: 气功 ; customary Chinese: 氣功 ; "pinyin: qìgōng; Wade–Giles: ch'i Kung;" plainly: "life-energy cultivation") is a general method of harmonious pose and drive, inhalation and reflection, used to train well-being, religiousness, and fighting arts. Rooted in Chinese medication, thinking, and fighting arts, qigong is considered the practice of cultivating and balancing qi (pronounced "qi"), traditionally translated as "vital energy" in China and Asia.

Qigong exercises usually include meditation movements, coordination of slow movements, deep rhythmic breathing, and calm mind meditation. In China and around the world, qigong is practiced for relaxation, bodybuilding, preventative drugs, self-medication, substitute medication, reflection, self-development, and martial arts exercise. Scientists inspected pores in terms of various diseases (including high blood pressure, pain, and cancer) and quality of life.

Chi (or qi) is often translated as vital energy and represents the energy that circulates throughout the physique. A further universal meaning is a general liveliness, comprising electromagnetic liveliness, heat, and light; Descriptions frequently include the relationship between gas, matter, breath or air, spirit, and energy. Qi is the most important opinion in customary Chinese medication and fighting arts. "Gong (or Kung Fu)" is regularly explained as self-development or development of labor, and meanings comprise exercise, skills, abilities, achievements, services, results or achievements and are usually performed in gong Fu (Kung Fu) in the logic of traditionally good achievements. These two words are combined to describe a system that processes and balances vital liveliness, specifically for good shape.

The word "pores," used today, has remained popularized to refer to various Chinese self-improvement movements and to emphasize healing and scientific approaches from the late 1940s to the 1950s. Focusing on spiritual practice, mysticism and elite perfection.

Benefits of Qigong

The pores are managed by "TCM," "CAM," "integrative medication," and some medical professionals. It is considered a "standard medical technique," pores are usually prescribed to treat various conditions, in China. Clinical uses include diabetes, menopause syndrome, chronic liver disease, peptic ulcer disease, hypertension, coronary heart disease, cancer, tumors, myopia, back and leg pain, obesity, insomnia, and cervical spondylosis. External parts of China, qigong can be used as an adjunct to medicines or as an adjunct to traditional methods of treatment, including relaxation, health, restoration, and healing of certain illnesses. Nonetheless, at hand, no qualitative indication that pores are truly operative in this condition. A systematic review of clinical trials suggests that, at the current level of evidence, it is not possible to determine the effectiveness of pores in certain diseases.

Safety and Cost

Porosity is generally considered safe. In clinical trials, side effects were not observed; the pores were considered safe for use in other groups. Minimum costs for self-management and high costs for managing the group. In general, the warnings associated with the stoma are similar to the risk of muscle deformities or strains, sprains to prevent injuries, general safety when used with existing medical procedures, and physical activity in consultation with a doctor. In combination with traditional medicine.

Intuitive Healing

Intuitive Energy Healing is a holistic healing approach that provides practitioners with access to their deep meditation conditions and altered awareness through alpha-theta and delta brainwaves that provide intuitive information about health or life. Practicing clients work with God to help change and change the emotions, beliefs, and energies that contribute to the imbalance. Intuitive energy healing can be used to create physical, emotional, spiritual, or mental healing.

How It Works

Intuitive energy therapists conduct self-meditation for several seconds in a state of delay (a change in the state of perception). In this state of meditation, practitioners may relate to superconscious or sacred thoughts about God, divine sources, etc. This full and complete communication with God allows practitioners to access and provide clients with intuitive or extrasensory reading. By reading this book, you can intuitively accept the physical, mental, emotional, or spiritual factors associated with your client's current problems.

Your faith is the matrix on which all reality is based. Faith is the energy that is the basis for creating your mind, your thoughts generate your emotions, and your emotions cause your actions and actions. Many intuitive approaches to energy healing with only that matrix - "secrets" that instantly change beliefs, can change your life! That is why I call it a "secret" secret.

The Secret Behind

The Secret movie teaches ancient wisdom that satisfies our thoughts and feelings create in our reality. This is true, but there are no elements in this image. I call this element "a secret hidden behind a secret." The answer lies in the material changes that create our thoughts and feelings in the matrix of trust. Your faith supports everything that you think, feel, and do, so the most effective way to start here is to change your behavior or lifestyle. Therefore, persuasion is a way to integrate and coordinate your thoughts and feelings. Intuitive healing is a special tool that can immediately change our faith. Only when we believe in work will we begin to change the source of reality from the source of creation.

Muscle testing and energy testing – Your intuitive doctor uses energy or muscle tests to test limited beliefs. Muscle testing is a simple technique used to effectively test a client's subconscious mind to determine if limited beliefs exist.

Download feelings and programs – Another important part of the intuitive treatment method is downloading certain emotions and programs from the creators. By downloading emotions and programs, you can teach your customers that they have such beliefs and fully accept them. For example, a practitioner may ask God or a source to impose on a client the belief that "I am rich," but if the client does not know what it means to be rich, it is unlikely that faith will last long. This may not work fully. Thus, the client can immediately feel at the cellular level what he is feeling. This will make it easier for customers to accept "new" beliefs at an unconscious level.

The Role of an Intuitive Healing Practitioner—Witnessing

What I like about this technique is that God / Source / Space is the main engine. The practitioner's role is to present the requested or proposed vocation or prayer and then witness the change. Witnessing is an integral part of the realization of healing, but it is God who does the real work. This differs from many other forms, which are highly dependent on the intention to move and manipulate energy as the healer wants. In intuitive treatment, the doctor can approach the highest vibration, unconditional love or god, the universe, the origin of God, etc.

The Seven Elevations of Consciousness

A metaphysical understanding of the structure of reality is seven spheres or seven consciousnesses. In fact, all levels are a manifestation of the same reality, but the concept of seven cats is useful for understanding how intuitive healing works, why it is different from others, and sometimes from others.

12 Strand DNA and DNA Activation

For decades, scientists have believed that only two strands of DNA are useful to us. They could not determine the function or purpose of ten additional strands, so they made the remaining ten strands of unwanted DNA. Now science confirms that this direction can have many goals. For spiritual healers, this junk DNA has a purpose! When 12 strands of DNA are activated, the body is ready for the next stage of evolution on Earth. DNA activation enhances our innate intuitive and mental abilities and helps our body get rid of the many poisons that we face today. Activated DNA can slow down the aging process by activating the so-called chromosomes and vitality. The chromosomes of youth and vitality are real "young glands" found somewhere other than our own DNA.

Clear Negative Energy

Intuitive treatments are effective in removing negative energy and effects on the body and inanimate objects such as houses and buildings. Souls, mental rings, wires, structures, and other energy effects can cause problems in everyday life. Worse, you may not even be aware that these "invisible" energies affect us. Radiation and other environmental islands can be removed from the body in a similar way. The doctor cleans all this by scanning the energy fields. Body Healing and Internal Observation: Medically Intuitive

You can also create physical healing using intuitive energy healing. Doctors observe changes in the body using the same connections as the gods, available through changing conditions of perception. Looking inside the body and communicating with various organ systems, doctors can get an idea and information about what can happen to the physical health of the patient. The term "medically intuitive" is that term. In general, trust comes from physical healing so that our clients are confident that they can accept and maintain a healthy state.

Manifesting Abundance

If you are looking for more abundance in your life, intuitive energy healing is also an amazing tool. The skills of self-expression and abundance in healing theta are very strong, such as financial abundance, finding a spouse, doing the best job. The work of faith and feelings is usually integrated into rich techniques that are easy to learn and apply.

Guardian Angels, Spirit Guides and the Deceased

Intuitive energy healing methods allow you to communicate with your guardian angel, spiritual guide, or a deceased relative. Sometimes, when God sends them as an important part of healing, these creatures automatically appear during the healing session. In spiritual healing, we can always come close to the energy of unconditional love (God, the Holy Spirit, source, etc.) before connecting with the mind of the keeper.

One Path Many Ways to Apply

In general, practitioners intuitively manage what should happen during the session. In general, many clone combinations are used for each session. Each session is completely intuitive, so each session is different. Intuitive energy healing works directly with this creative force, which we understand as creative forces such as

God/Universe/Source, so our customers always get the best and best at the moment.

Spiritual Healing

Curing is frequently a combination of intermediations such as bodily, non- medicinal, violent surgery, and cerebral surgery. As soon as we change the source of the illness or overcome and overawed the difficult, we focus on curing. Curing is a full bundle. If you study just 1 component of the disease, then there will be very little recovery. In divine curing, the history of medication is created that consists of healing processes and places of healing. Spiritual recipes for the physique, mind, and soul and begin the path of healing, is created.

The Journey of Spiritual Healing

The path of spiritual healing refers to spiritual, mental, emotional, and physical poisons. Now this tactic, we remove the poison that pollutes the humanity. Then and there it provokes movement from someone and from oneself. You can do both. Soul healing is a combination of healing stages for the physique, mind, and soul. Several of us contemplate an act and then execute other acts. For instance, we contemplate we need to inscribe the present and actually go to the seashore. Otherwise, we have serious requirements, and we are moving physically in different directions. This happens to most of us every day.

Do Your Body Right

Consume Well. "What Does It Mean For Us Now? Is it possible to eat less sugar? Are we still eating fast food? Do you drink enough water?" Discover a little way to mend your eating behaviors. Consume extra root vegetables. Consume extra organic and local foodstuffs.

Practice finding fun, easy-to-integrate exercises in our day-to-day lives is one of the principal encounters that have various facades. Do what you want to dance, walk, surf, jump, swim, do yoga, and do whatever you want!

Take care of your body. Massage or spend your health with friends. Go to your chiropractor or physiotherapist. Find a healing circle that heals the body and responds to complaints that may be active.

Sleep

" Are you getting enough sleep? Do we feel rested?" Get enough rest switch off the television. Yield it overnight and wet the candle.

If our bodies are well taken care of, it usually restores our hearts and minds! Over time, you need to start and build your workouts so that they are easy to maintain and scale. We can always do something for the body!

Purify Your Relationship

"What does it mean to cleanse our hearts, relationships, and personal energy fields? Do you give and receive intimate relationships? Or are you doing your best? Or did you just get this?"

Practice love without judgment. When it is right and wrong to compare and judge others constantly, the heart cannot be pure. Find a trainer or help desk consultant to help you make the decision.

Growth Consciousness about, Building and Maintaining your Liveliness. We get exposure to lethal liveliness at workplaces, in interactions, and also from the Internet and television. First of all, reduce the negative liveliness that you get day in day out, now find some good activities that aid in maintaining and building liveliness. Acupuncture, qigong, and light visuals are only a few practices.

Use the Mind for Creative Freedom

"How do we free our hearts and use them to grow and create the life we love?" Exercise reflection. Here are various special ways to meditate in order to keep the mind clean. Here are many types of reflection. Attempt some of them and exercise what attracts your body, mind, and mind the most!

Follow the development of intellectual tasks. Find ways to read, take courses, graduate, and build your mind.

I tell a story. I am my own story. Write and tell your stories. Test your thoughts.

Liberate Your Soul from Ego

"How can we free the soul?" The soul is connected with the body, mind, and mind. They do not fight alone. Therefore, if you find your favorite movement for the body, mind, mind, the soul will be liberated. You will experience more moments when your thoughts are in harmony with the physical feelings and movements of your body.

Where to wake up. Be prepared to strengthen your mystical depth hence that you enclose biting bulk without discomfort, liveliness to attain your dreams and a clear intelligence for decision-making without interruption without hesitation. This will allow your soul to make the life you love!

Daily audits and practices. Make sure your practice is still relevant to your thoughts. "Are you starting to feel like zombies as a result of exercise?" perhaps its stage to crack fresh exercises or expand your training!

Commence the Spiritual Trip

When you practice to keep your body healthy and happy, balance your emotions and energies, and keep your mind clean and clear, sometimes spiritual aspects of illness, anxiety, and disharmony arise. Our powers can benefit from spiritual intervention.

Charge the battery. In shamanistic culture, it must be powerful. Power gives us the opportunity to be the author of our lives (and not the instructions of other individuals). One feature to recondition the authorization of a family, person, or the public is to fix up the way of animal detach.

Remove the improperly installed power source. Near is no competent or regretful liveliness. This is not the place where energy should be, but it should not move. The liveliness rehearses that your request will aid nevertheless if it cannot be ready to lend a hand to access a shaman so that he can carry the energy entering the body.

Remove parts for lost souls. When we experience injuries in life, we leave the country to protect ourselves from injuries. This is called the death of people in the shamanistic culture. Soul extraction is a shamanic way to recover lost souls so that we can recover.

Reunite with your ancestors. Know the mountain. It is important that we stand on the shoulders of others and are rooted in it. Otherwise, we risk being cruel. Relations with our family, friends, and ancestors those who love us are very important in every medical history. Previous ancestral treatment over the past 100 years often helps solve physical problems that they cannot solve.

Bright spiritual healing with light is an intercultural technique of spiritual healing that helps to change the negative and poison around us and around us. If your body, mind, and mind can become more balanced and harmonized over time and remove stones laid in light groups, you will find that you can keep your core strong and energetic. Walk the life of light, shine brightly, and inspire others to dive deeper into their light.

Often, more than one intervention is required to treat and improve everyday life. This is a fatal way to make a big story for our loved ones and us and lives a consistent and meaningful life.

Magnetic Field Therapy

Magnetic therapy supports overall health by using various types of magnets throughout the body. It may also help in the treatment of certain diseases. At hand are a number of types, counting

Static Magnetic Field Therapy

This way, you affect the membrane with a magnet. You can friction a captivating armlet or other alluring jewelry. This bottle can be a magnetic dressing or the use of a magnet as the sole for shoes. Besides, have a siesta on a unique mattress with a lure.

Electrically Charged Magnetic Therapy (Electromagnetic Therapy)

The magnet used here is electrically charged. Treatment with electromagnetic therapy is usually done with electrical stimulation.

Its Workings

Your physique obviously has an alluring handle and an exciting field. Each molecule contains a minor quality of captivating loveliness. The crucial model of compelling therapy is that sure harms arise due to an imbalance of magnetic fields. It is assumed that if you bring the magnetic field closer to your body, everything will return to square one. Ions, such as potassium and calcium, aids cell mails signals. In the course of the tests, researcher's aphorism how magnets convert the exert yourself of ions. But accordingly, significantly at hand is no sign that the magnet has the same effect on the cell when it is in the cell.

Uses

Most magnetic therapy is an option for treating various types of pain, including:

Inflammation ache Twisting curing Sleeplessness

Head pains Fibromyalgia ache

It's harmless for many individuals to put on a low-intensity motionless magnet, but magnetic therapy is not good at the time of the following:

Are using a pacer Possess an insulin thrust Are expectant

All magnets must be removed before an MRI or x-rays. Other individuals receiving self-medication have the following side effects:

Ache

Queasiness Faintness

These effects are infrequent.

Workability

There is not a lot of self-healing researches. Created people do not have enough data to make a reasonable conclusion. Although some clinical studies have revealed the possibility of self-healing, such as treatment for lower back pain, there is no clear evidence that any disease can be treated.

Polarity Therapy

Polarity Therapy is a comprehensive liveliness-based structure that comprises recommendations for your body, nutrition, exercise, and lifestyle to restore and maintain the body's proper energy flow. The basic conception of polar therapy is that completely the liveliness of the individual amount is based on electromagnetic liveliness and the illness is the result of improper use of energy.

An Australian-American chiropractor, osteoporosis therapist, and alternative physician, Randolph Stone (1888-1981), developed polar therapy integrating East-West principles and treatments. During his stay in India, he learned the olden ideologies of "Ayurvedic philosophy." In search of the basics of individual vitality, he premeditated reflexology and herbal medication. He studied reflexology and herbal medicine.

Stone is dedicated to the principles of Ayurvedic medicine, interpreted in connection with scientific and medical discoveries for the definition of polar therapy. According to an Ayurvedic philosophy based on fixed ideologies known as The Trident, the liveliness of the mortal physique focuses on five organs or areas (large intestines, lungs, small intestines, diaphragm, heart region, and brain). One of the five forms of air or liveliness controls each area: "prana" of the mind, veins of the lungs and heart, diaphragm, small Adana of the small intestine, and pain in the colon. Five rays regulate the movement of all directions of the body; each air indicates its movement. Stone also discovered that cerebral prana ultimately regulates the combined forces of the body. Violations or restrictions of pranic blood flow, thus, affect the well-being of the whole organism. The power of "prana" is facilitated by the stream of air and food into the physique, interaction with additional breathing creatures, and the absorption of the five senses.

He spent a lot of time on detailed and detailed causal relationships between human anatomy and disease, based on the flow of vital energy. He also connected electromagnetic energy to an energy source. The medical symbol is used as a medicine symbol to determine the nature of the flow on the diagram of the human body and to describe in detail the movement of energy. Polar therapy is based on a graphical flow of energy. The basic energy model is determined by the spiral movements that occur in the navel and determines the initial energy flow of the uterus.

Benefits of Polarity Healing

Polarity healing releases and replenishes the stream of vital liveliness and eliminates the disease, restoring the balance of unbalanced energy. The patient learns to relieve stress by controlling stressors and acting accordingly.

This treatment can improve the health and healing of all those who seek a decent lifestyle. It has been reported that polar healing is operative for anybody exposed/unprotected from toxic poison. Similarly, HIV-infected patients may feel comfortable in polar therapy. It is also suitable for:

Releasing overall tension Vertebral ache

Stomach pains

Other repeated illnesses and disorders

How It Works

After defining the precise cause of the client's liveliness inequity, the specialist commences running the first session of a sequence of physical work periods aimed at training and relieving the client of incorrect guidance. Therapy, such as massage, is based on energy pressure and includes blood circulation. During treatment, the therapist draws thoughtfulness to the force exerted on every point, even if limb pressure is applied to the anatomical points of each patient. Combining the central scheme or focus of polar therapy, this technique is very soft and unique to polar therapy. To stimulate the energy of the body, it captures subtle strains and skulls. Despite the intense and deep pressure used with massage techniques, polar therapists never come in contact with them.

To help the body, the therapist often prescribes a diet for the disposal and disposal of food waste from patients. The rules of polar healing take into account certain connections amid diverse foodstuffs and mortal liveliness arenas. In the same way, a series of exercises is often determined. This exercise, called Yogin polarity, includes squats, stretching, periodic actions, profound inhalation, and voice manifestation. They could irritate plus soothe. On request, counseling can be provided as part of a very personalized treatment plan to improve stability.

Before starting treatment, each patient has a complete medical history. Such preliminary oral examinations often monopolize the first treatment session. In some situations, the therapist may need to evaluate your body stability over scrutiny and bodily inspection.

Safety

Polar healing is harmless for almost everyone because of the inherent gentleness of massage therapy, including the elderly and the weak.

This therapy involves the release of very emotional liveliness (tears, laughter, or both combined).

Research and Acceptance

It is an adjunctive therapy for holistic spiritual therapy that can be used with a medicinal method. Polar healing is adept globally, but most specialists are located around the US. Present-day researchers use notions related to the simple theory of stone reality to define quantum void (QV) as the basis of all reality. But in 2000, this holistic system did not yet reach the widespread recognition that Stone expected in 1981 before he died.

This is an adjunctive therapy for complex spiritual therapy that can be used with medical approaches. Polar healing is exercised globally, but most specialists are located in the United States. Present-day researchers use notions related to the elementary theory of mountain reality to define quantum leakage (QV) as the basis of all reality. But in 2000, this holistic system was not widely recognized as what Stone hoped for in 1981.

Practitioner

"The American Association for Polarity Therapy (APTA)" permits two stages of education. "Associate Polarity Specialist (APP)" is an initial step grounded on the least stage of knowledge. Registered polar practices (RPPs) are assigned to graduates in a recognized curriculum. Graduate and special education is offered in various fields, and APTA provides certification to practitioners.

Chakra

Chakra translates as "Rad." The seven chakras of the body are other energy centers that begin in the upper part of the head and end in the spine. They regulate every part of the system and affect everything from emotional processing to disease resistance.

In general, the seven chakra meditation techniques focus on opening and aligning the chakra. If they are blocked or not synchronized, they can affect their physical and mental health.

After adjusting the position of the chakra, you can open the chakra and develop an intuition about a blockage. This will help you identify and solve problems that arise before they lead to serious consequences. You can also do what you need to find and remove old wounds. In short, healing can occur through proper knowledge of the chakras.

The chakra system began in India between 1500 and 500 BC. The oldest text of the Veda says: "Reiki's healer and yoga teacher Fern Olivia. The Vedas are the earliest Sanskrit literary record and the oldest Hindu scriptures. What is the purpose of the seven chakras? "Affects the emotional, mental, emotional and spiritual life and all areas of your life," Olivia said. "This chakra contains either prana or the best pure healing energy around us. The study of the location of the chakras (meditation, reiki or yoga) is based on the belief that our energy flows freely and prana can pass through it when the chakra is open and parallel. "

Root Chakra What It Is
Imagine the root chakra (the first aka chakra) as the base of the house,

separate from the body. It maintains and protects everything while it is solid, stable, and working properly. According to Olivia, this is due to the spine, the first three vertebrae, and the pelvic floor and is in charge of the logic of safety and human existence. Consequently, this applies to everything that you use on earth, including basic requirements comprising of security, water, food, and shelter, together with several emotive desires, comprising of a sense of anxiety and security. As we all have knowledge that, you do not need to worry too much when these requirements are met.

When It Is Blocked

Fans say that various diseases can be caused by various reasons, comprising of anxiety conditions, worries, or bad dreams. Bodily, the first chakra is allied with complications of the legs or feet, colon, excretion or vertebral, bladder.

The Sacral Chakra What Is It

Think of the second chakra as the funniest of the seven. Olivia is said to be above the belly and under the navel and is responsible for our sexual and creative energy. Most convenient if the sacred chakras are aligned with elements of orange and water. It is friendly, vibrant, and successful, and at the same time evokes a feeling of well-being, satiety, pleasure, and pleasure. (Fun!) Keep moving the energy wheel, changing your body, and creatively expressing yourself.

When It Is Blocked

If you are inspired by creativity or experiencing emotional instability, the sacred chakra may not have been adjusted. In addition, this may be due to physical, sexual dysfunction, possibly dread of transformation, misery, or behavioral addiction.

The Solar Plexus Chakra What Is It

Its name means "shining stone" in Sanskrit. The third chakra (now it should

not be confused with the sixth chakra, the "third eye") should be a source of individual power over self-esteem. Or, as Olivia said: "A chakra based on behavior and balance that focuses on individual will, personal strength, and dedication." It is believed that from the navel to the chest, it solves all the problems of metabolism, digestion, and stomach health.

When It Is Blocked

You may be worse. It is difficult for you to make decisions, to have problems with anger or control. Olivia not only feels bad, but also indicates that she can express outward apathy, doubt, or easily be beneficial. Similarly, several types of abdominal pain can occur: Like digestive problems or gas. (UV).

The Heart Chakra What It Is

The same applies to Chopra, since the mid chakra, this is the number four chakra in the middle of the rib cage, is the site of physical and mental encounters. The body should include the thymus (that plays an important part in the lymphatic and endocrine systems), chest, lungs, and heart. And as the name implies, everything is connected with love. "This is spiritual awareness, forgiveness, and the awakening of service," Olivia said. In terms of green and pink (yes, millennial types of rose quartz), when the heart chakra is balanced and stable, I think affection and love stream easily. "Good vibration is almost contagious," Olivia said.

When It Is Blocked
A closed chakra can give way to unhappiness, fury, possessiveness, a dread of treachery and hatred of oneself and other people, particularly fear of someone or somebody. Causing pain has negative emotions that lead you away from the possibility of love.

Throat Chakra What It Is
How do you feel? The fifth chakra, which tells the inner truth or allows you to convey the inner truth correctly, can be balanced. The throat chakra controls all communications and, according to Olivia, is the first of three spiritual chakras (in contrast to the appearance of the bottom). Anatomically, the pharynx of the chakra is connected to the parathyroid gland, thyroid gland, mouth, jaw, tongue, larynx, and neck. If there is a

positivity in this chakra, you can clearly hear, speak, and express yourself.

When It Is Blocked

Although it's easy to tell the truth, it's hard to pay attention to others, focus on others, or be afraid of punishing other people. Actually, this obstruction could be evident as thyroid problems, aching throat, stiffness in the neck and shoulders, or tension headaches.

The Third Eye Chakra What Is It

Do not confuse the name. The third eye chakra is actually the number six chakra and is actually positioned amid the eyebrows. Body parts, including the eyes, lower brain, head and pituitary should be controlled by the third eye. And it must be able to control intuition, recognize and use it. In addition, the third eye should be responsible for everything between you and the outside world, acting as a bridge between two images so that you can carve fantasies and dramas to see clear images.

When It Is Blocked

It may be difficult for you to approach intuition, believe in that inward opinion, remember vital particulars, or learn fresh abilities. And when the lower chakras (sacrum, sacrum, solar plexus and AKA heart chakra) go out of balance, this may be the third eye, which looks more condemned, disgusting and closed. Third eye blocking is connected to a variety of problems, comprising of misery, unease, and more judgment. However, he claims to physically cause headaches, dizziness, and various other head condition problems.

The Crown Chakra What Is It

According to the Chopra Center, this place, known in Sanskrit as the Sahasvara chakra or the Thousand Petals chakra, is the center of our higher self, others, and, finally, with God, enlightenment and spiritual connection. Just like the title proposes, it is the chakra number seven and is positioned on the peak of the head. Transformations that occur internally during synchronization are called pure recognition, recognition, non-separation, and extension lines. Mostly more than you and part of the universe.

When It Is Blocked

Blocking the crown chakra allows you to feel isolation or emotional pain— the main feeling that everything and everyone excludes. Or you feel like a normal self, but you are spiritually connected, and not in a state of sublime enlightenment. This is very nice and ordinary. Contrary to the other chakras, it usually completely opens with specific yoga exercises, meditation exercises, or a specific time. This is not a specific method that can be applied at any time. However, through daily practice, you can taste it through meditation, prayer, moments of silence and thanksgiving, and even spiritual relationships.

How to Unlock Chakra

There are several methods you can use to learn how to unlock chakras. Your energy path is not only clean, but your balance and harmony are restored. It also offers all the benefits of an open and flowing vitality.

Mantra

Short repetitions of mantras are often used as the beginning and end of yoga practice. Mantras are also practiced in various prayer ceremonies in monasteries and individual religious practices. The sounds of spells vibrate in the chest, lower abdomen, or neck in the form of healing sounds, creating an energy model that turns the energy field back into health.

According to the Chopra Center, if you use Mala, there are usually several repetitions of your order if you need to repeat the order. Hold the hammer in one hand to calculate how many times the spell is repeated.

Select a Mantra

Select the order or series of orders that you want to sing. Using mantras during meditation can draw attention to random thoughts. In the Vedic tradition, practitioners use bija mantras to cleanse and balance the chakras.

Each mantra is a separate syllable corresponding to a particular chakra. When you sing, open each syllable and focus on the erased chakra and feel the mantra that the chakra sings.

Root - LAM (pronounced lahm) Sacral - VAM (pronounced vahm)

Solar Plexus - RAM (pronounced rahm)

Heart - YAM (pronounced yahm) Throat - HAM (pronounced hahm)

Third eye - OM (pronounced ohm or Aum) Crown - silence

You can also use vocals to erase the chakras. Expand each vocal to make it a song.

"Root chakra" - "Uh" like duh "Sacral chakra" - "Oo" like you

"Solar plexus chakra" - "Oh" like go

"Heart chakra" - "Ah" like craw "Throat chakra" - "Eye" like cry

"Third eye chakra" - "Ay" like say "Crown chakra" - "Eee" like bee

How to Use Mantra When Meditating

Choose a quiet place to the side. Choose a warm place where the rhythm of the body slows down, and body temperature can drop. Sit on the floor or cross your legs to meditate. Take three deep breaths to relax. Keep calm and talk about your intention to meditate, for example, step on the chakra or keep it in balance. Keep your hands on your hips or extended. If you use a rosary, hold each hand and repeat each ball to count each ball. Repeat your order in 9 groups. Breathe naturally, but be careful with breathing. Focus on vocals and visualize chakra of repeated spells. Finish your meditation by repeating scabies or other favorite songs.

Tapping

Eavesdropping or Emotional Freedom Technique (EFT) technology is best described by Nick and Jessica Ortner, one of the founders of the Tapping Solution Foundation. A prerequisite is the repeated touch of the fingertip at a certain point on the meridian. When you listen, repeat the words of gratitude and accept the emotions associated with the memory. Such feelings can affect the chakras and energy systems throughout the body.

Tapping Chakra Points

Amy B. Sher, one of the most important psychic, physical, and spiritual healers, explains that EFT can be used to open chakras. Time (see Chakra Image above for chakra points). Launch the crown chakra and continue to touch it nine times to the roots. Combine the bit with the order above if desired.

Reiki

Reiki Master works with symbolic and manual positions to deliver Reiki energy. After the necessary preparation and attention of the Reiki Master, the doctor may order reiki to open the blocked center of the chakra and release a stream of energy. You can also take advantage of Reiki processing using remote Reiki processing technology. If you are familiar with reiki, try activating the chakra by touching each energy center for three to five minutes. Or visit a Reiki specialist and ask him to focus on cleansing the chakra.

How Reiki Unlocks

Reiki energy is literally like a burst of high energy that moves and is removed through the chakra. According to the Reiki International Education Center, the introduction of reiki, a positive energy field, raises and removes negative blocking vibrations. This negative energy cannot support negative vibration levels and degrades performance.

Yoga

Yoga can open the chakra, stimulating this energy center, manipulating the several portions of the physique associated with the chakra, through the movement of the yoga pose. For example, there are five yoga chakra poses that you can practice to unlock a locked energy center.

Blocked Chakra

A blocked chakra does not stop spinning. It can also be burned like flesh. The chakra can restore natural torque instead of turning it off. None of these answers are healthy or desirable. Each of these conditions negatively affects you, because the chakra is the door to the vital energy flowing through your body.

Learning How to Unblock A Chakra

There are many methods that you can use to unlock the chakras. Try a few methods to discover the technology that does it well in you, and practice it regularly to keep your energy center open and increase your energy flow.

Chapter 3 More About Energy Healing

Benefits of Energy Healing

One of the most common remuneration of liveliness curing is relaxation and stress cut; this triggers the physiques effortless remedial abilities and maintains and improves well-being.

Liveliness curing is a native therapy that balances the physiques life-force gently and bring as well-being and health to the recipient.

The remedial of the liveliness coldness is conceded out manually the surge of liveliness to the client is possible by an energy healer. This is a very strong, but gentle energy sent intentionally. When the life stream stops, weakens, or is blocked, emotional or health problems can occur. In many situations, such as emotional or physical trauma, trauma, anxiety, anxiety, suspicion, anger, anxiety, negative self-talk, addiction, malnutrition, emotional or physical trauma, including a devastating lifestyle, trauma, negative thoughts and feelings. And the lack of relationships, neglect and love of other individuals and yourself because of sentiments that are not articulated in a fit method.

Healing liveliness can sound somewhat depressing. Sometimes people ask: "But what can cause healing with energy?" The benefits of healing energy can be at some stage: physical, spiritual, mental, emotional or vital. It could be theatrical, but regularly refined. They could occur instantly, but come in the future when a curing period is going.

Regularly, "results" arise at a stage that provides the greatest benefit. The main advantage of a healing session (or healing session) can be, for example, an understanding or change in attitude that leads to behavioral changes that continuously improve emotional health, physical health and / or value of lifetime.

Thanks to the personal experience of donors and recipients of energy, healing energy can benefit from:

Better Stress Management
What if you tend not only to cope well with stressful situations, but also to wear them? Stress does not arise in such a situation, but in how it is dealt with. And the way you deal with situations often depends more on the unresolved feelings that they aroused in the past. Past situations where someone feels useless, helpless, shy or

unloved can destroy cellular memory. All trauma is not inherent to you, but to those who color the entire future experience. Energy therapy can dissolve cellular memory to increase your ability to think clearly and find solutions that no longer experience past situations. Stephanie solves this problem through a series of Reiki sessions. When they first met, he was so excited that he asked until his lips were growing. But after many sessions, he played without chewing his lips.

It's better not to take full advantage of this situation, because it releases old energy. Remember that you attract only external experiences that correspond to your inner self.

Better Self-care

The more energy you get, the more you take care of it. As the best energy flows through you, you will feel better. Andronicus experienced this on himself. The Reiki phase focused on it also provides for other practitioners (note: it is important for therapists to continue to receive support). Diet. Finally, he decided to get rid of refined sugar and as a result lost 40 kilograms.

Better Relationships

Regardless of whether we know it or not, our interpretation of what others say or do is based on the past. In general, an experience for one of my favorite childhood years. For example, as we know, my boss is very similar to the mother of my client, so I have a client who cannot compare with my boss. Each time my boss speaks critically, my client returns to feelings of child abuse from an unstable mother. The only way to improve my boss's relationship with my client is to solve my mother's old trauma.

Better Creativity and Productivity

True creation does not come from our mind. Our mind is a tool for influencing divine inspiration, interpretation and understanding. To be creative, you must believe that you deserve to be connected with God. You must believe that you are capable. You should not be attached to what other people think of you. You should think that you have all the support and resources needed to complete the production. Even if others are looking for time and attention to their goals, you should think of it as important enough to devote time and attention to them.

Emotional memories that cannot judge or judge your creation can interfere with all these needs. Disabling this cellular memory will allow renewing this channel for energy treatment, making it more creative and successfully completing the project.

Better Intuition

The same channel that stimulates creativity also contributes to intuition. If you want to speak with an angel, an ascended teacher, a deceased relative, or the source of God, you must believe that you are worthy and capable. No matter what you do, in the eyes of God or in "affirmation," you also must not limit your faith. Everything that causes healing energy provides creativity and intuition.

Better Ease and Happiness

These benefits combine, but happiness is the norm. Laugh more and laugh more. Your views and expectations are more positive. They expect something to happen to you easily. The betrayal of the universe is the betrayal of the universe. Because I understand and believe how the universe works, and I feel happy and calm when the universe does it.

If you exceed this threshold, you no longer have to worry about returning to your old ways. And it doesn't take long to get there! It took several years, but since energy flows faster, I realized that my clients who have been in therapy older than 6 months are a lot happier and at ease. And I also learned to support those who are not yet in this state.

Better Real Life Magic and Manifestation

The law of attraction is written beyond the threshold of happiness without this confusion; it reacts with happier things. Impulse develops and experiences more and more motivation. You better know it and use it. Your life begins to feel magic.

This is how life can be for you. Perhaps the short-term benefits of steps 1-6 will feel busy right now, but it won't take long to start seeing the eight signs of miracles in life until you reach standard seven of new happiness. If you continue to use it, this result is guaranteed because it is the desired result, simple, synchronous and truly magical.

Natural relief or reduction of pain (or especially chronic pain relief, pain-related changes)

It's easier to deal with stressful situations.

It improves the health of the immune system - it is more resistant to diseases and recovers faster than from diseases and injuries.

Healing energy also provides the extra energy needed to recover from illness.

Bigger brains of emotional wellness absorbed feel of serenity and calm

Emotional let loose and curative

Enhanced mental clarity free of blocked energy Chakra healing, balancing, and payment

Balancing of energy

relief of deep, persistent muscle tension relief of nervousness relief from and better resistance to frequent mild depression education enhanced creativity, creative production, and badly behaved solving enhanced public insight accelerated personality increase and/or spiritual evolution emotional make public and curing enhanced mental clarity

Energy Remedial

Since energy therapy is indeed an additional cure, it could also be cast-off as an additional treatment. This supplements and improves the upkeep that patients receive in hospitals or some medical facilities.

Healing energy supplements western and eastern medication, and everyone could advantage. It's good for the well-being of females (including expectant women), males and kids, it is good for faunas (horses, dogs, and cats), water, plants, etc.

Healing Energy is an instrument that helps you relieve stress, relieve pain and quickly receive energy anytime, anywhere.

If we are calm and not stressed, we can restore natural healing abilities. If a person is healthy, regular treatment of hernias increases the body's defenses. This is manifested in harmony with external trust when working with everyday events. Man shows a positive attitude towards life.

Facts That Can Get Rid of Confusion and Misunderstanding Regarding Healing Energy

Healing Energy is Grounded on Scientific Philosophies

In high school we learnt physics, and everyone learns that matter comprises of particles. Some solid objects, including lumps, always vibrate. As humans, we also vibrate. When someone says that they have "good vibrations," they are speaking about the energy vibration of that person, that is, a happy person who shakes at higher frequencies. You can feel the spirit! There is also vibration in the seat. When you enter the room you just met, you can feel a strong energy and leave immediately. On the beach, light is through salty (an ordinary energy purifier) and poignant air. Beach air vibrates at higher frequencies.

Cultures Have Premeditated the Physique's Energy Hubs for Decades

Reiki is a custom of curing Japanese energy that began at the beginning of the 20th century. The Chakra, the center of the s7 energy transfers of the physique, is depicted in olden Hindu manuscripts. The body's liveliness path, the Meridian, is a roadmap for practitioners of traditional Chinese medicine to create acupuncture. In other ancient cultures, various forms were used to stimulate the body's natural healing abilities, but everyone regarded interior liveliness as a good energy.

You Don't Partake of to be Spiritual to Profit from Energy Remedial

Right like you don't hardship to realize the bylaw of gravity before falling, you don't basic to altogether appreciate the perception of full of life curative before being absorbed. For maximum benefit, it is advisable to enter with an open mind. It is always a bright idea to go to a liveliness therapist. If you've got stress, anxiety, or physical fatigue, healing energy sessions could aid you to be at ease and have an impression of stability. If you have a good feeling already, you can at all times get a bit improved! It should be noted that healing energy is an additional method that should not exclude affordable Western medicines.

Healing Energy Is Absolutely Available

Many are types of liveliness therapy devices that you could get anywhere. There are Reiki specialists in the globe, and the attractiveness of caring for Reiki is that they could give and receive, regardless of if they are in the similar room or not. Why? The supremacy of intent permits energy to stream to where desirable.

Acupuncture is easily available, but the client should be in front of the needle. This form arouses the stream of qi to balance the physique.

Another way to stimulate the meridian is through reflexology, tissues and structures through the parts of the legs, arms and ear, release blocked energy and promote healing.

Even massage is a method of energy healing, because it can relieve muscle tension, increase lymph flow and relax deeply.

If you are not familiar with this practice, contact a well-known specialist. Ask your yoga studio or friend for alternative medicine. Start a short 30- minute Reiki session and you will feel how powerful the healing energy is.

Your Energetic Health Can Be Maintained at Home

Like you take a bath every day and get your teeth brushed, cleaning energy should work every day. After visiting an energy therapist, if you begin to feel that your weight is returning back to your body, take a bath for 20 minutes with Epsom salt or pink Himalayan salt to allow vibration to flow. Staining or burning the sage's surrounding car will also remove any negative energy. High-quality crystal has its particular curative possessions and could enhance the liveliness arena. To start your energy healing journey all you require is inquisitiveness and a desire to study. How do you can break!

Reasons to Try Energy Healing

This reminds you that you are programmed to develop in any country where you grew up in divorce, harassment or insecurity. But first you need to erase all the "dirty" energy accumulated in your body. Every thought, action or action that you take is printed on the field of energy or aura. You blush and squeeze negative thinking, making this energy closer to your body. This thinking creates nerve trails in the head. This is also manifested by emotional, mental or physical pain.

What then if you can get rid of network problems? What if you could focus on more positive thoughts and reveal who you are? Energy therapy can remove "dirt" from the energy field. You can develop anyone before you! Here are 5 ways to use healing energy.

It dispels tension and strain to permit profound easing.

Stress is felt not only in the head, but throughout the body. EFT (Emotional Freedom) or printing technology is an effective way of persuading. By stimulating the meridian of a chiropractor, we say that the brain is safe to rest.

It reliefs liveliness obstructions so that you have an impression of energetic lightness and happiness.

The entirety universe, containing humans, is trembling. We vibrate beams of vigor. A liveliness therapist will aid you get stationary and stagnant liveliness. Make your life wider and happier in just one session. In most cases, you may not be aware that you are carrying less energy until it is gone.

The ability of the body to naturally heal is accelerated and escalates vigor.

Healing energy is in addition to customary medicinal practice shouldn't be used to exclude homeopathic medicines. Unilateral energy therapy can help with universal energy tubes. The energy therapist opens in such a way that energizes the client's body. It is believed that this energy activates your own healing system.

Clears mental thought and negative emotional patterns.

Unsaid feelings could enter the physique matter. Experiencing what occurred during the past and worrying about the forthcoming makes the yogi call "chitta vrit" or speak monkeys in the mind. If this conversation doesn't take a lot of time to ruminate or quiet your thoughts, then blockages arise. Like this lump with a small dam on a vibrant river. When energy cannot efficiently stream over this zone, you usually have an impression that you're stuck and wonder if you can completely eliminate such thoughts and feelings.

Helps with prolonged health problems, ache relieving and acute injuries.

The normal form of the body is well-being and vitality. He identifies the cure automatically. This extraordinary mind works regardless of your mind. The light of the body often shows what we must do, and still must learn. When energy gets to the point of attention, it's a prevailing strength. Healing energy stimulates and activates the physique's normal healing powers. Vertebral ache could be a bodily expression of anxiety associated with endurance problems. Dissipating the chakras and kidneys from this block could be very helpful over time.

How It Works

Traditional energy healing falls into the category of cycle / intuitive magic. This is one of the simplest forms of magic training, and we all do it instinctively.

Black Magic

The word "black" means that black objects absorb energy and produce energy in the same way. The word "white" means that energy is released just as the sun emits light. To heal, give and receive someone technically always working together is black and white.

Magic can be used to steal human energy, but this is not a tool flaw, as you can use a knife to cut vegetables or threaten people. Since the sword itself is bad, man has no intention of having it. Black magic can be used to protect people undergoing surgery from attacks, etc., as described in previous articles on martial magic.

For further healing, you will need black magic (man) on the dark side to trigger a higher energy field to get rid of parasites and implants, which will be explained later in this article. This is enough for other forms of magic. The rest of this article will focus on healing energy.

Basics of Energy Healing

To cure energy, do this with appropriate symbolic measures. This is a fantastic way to say that you need to do something, touch someone or think about your intentions. Symbolic actions cannot be anything else, they can run away with the intention of healing someone, but they can distract. Therefore, a symbolic action must be something that can maintain focus while maintaining focus. You tried too much. It should flow naturally.

The standard for good doctors is what really matters to them. If this is really important to you, and you can feel the love of strangers, then you are a good doctor. If not, then only care about close friends and family. You can be a good doctor if you want. There is no problem. Not everyone needs to be a healer. Each has its own role. It will be a boring world where everyone is the same. Positive / beloved thoughts / warnings will give the person healing energy. That is why we are all regularly treated. But with more direct intentions and concentration, he becomes stronger.

Attunement/Initiation

It should not be cured or started in any way. However, there may be advantages and disadvantages. All treatments are effective and heal all energy. The difference is in technique or frame. A wireframe is a set of beliefs, structures, and skills.

The study of certain treatment methods has the advantage of providing access to the beliefs, structures and fundamentals of this method. For example, in Reiki, you will believe that you will be treated simultaneously with the character (we will look at the character later) and the recipient. It gives you a head. But the disadvantage is that it also limits the scope. It's like a martial arts study. All are good, but mixed martial arts are better because they have more choices. And over time, everyone develops a style that suits them.

In particular, relationships and initiations are a kind of energy transfer in which the teacher unknowingly shares his healing skills with you. These skills are inherent in the goal of completing consciousness. Honestly, whatever the consciousness itself, actual actions and part of consciousness symbolize the transfer and receipt of technologies invested in common energy. But you do not need it, you can practice and come.

How It Works

Any action is a ritual. The action symbolizes the amount of energy (time is energy, movement is energy, emotion is energy) that you are putting into the intention. It also symbolizes/proves that you actually mean it — if you say that you're healing someone but you don't dare to put your hands close to them then you obviously don't dare to enter their energy field, so it's not going work. For example, it's easy for most people to say "I love you," but to buy flowers you need to go out and bring flowers. The action symbolizes the amount of energy that you give to others.

Hand signals also have a value that already exists. Both exist materially and immaterially, like words. The word "table" has a real meaning that already exists, but you can agree to use the new word with your friends, and it works if everyone agrees. You can also decide with your friends that the word "table" now means "chair" and works if everyone agrees. The laying on of hands may mean, for example, "stop." Hand digging carelessly. Culturally, we agree. It functions perfectly as a ritual, because it miraculously shakes hands and knows what it means, as if committing something similar to a secret and a secret.

The longer and harder the mind, the better. However, this applies only to the moment when the amount of physical time and energy invested in the consciousness coincides with the amount of energy, according to the intention of people that the continuation of consciousness is ineffective, which makes people feel uncomfortable. People are worried that people are beginning to suspect that they are doing more than you say.

Physical Presence and Remote Healing

To treat someone, you need some kind of connection. A physical being is a relationship similar to a relationship with this person. This means that you can treat someone you don't know when you are physically, only someone who is far away from you. To relate to someone you need to find spiritually, you need to think about whether you know what WhatsApp is (the Internet is basically a copy of the spiritual world, so the same rules apply). With them, wherever they are (if any). To get WhatsApp for this person, you need to interact with him to share something like a conversation. Therefore, you should not randomly treat people whom you have never touched. However, you can treat any people who have just made Skype calls within 5 minutes.

Some people can find people spiritually and can communicate with the people they hear without speaking directly. You can do this the same way you can search for someone on the Internet or request a number without actually meeting. But this is not the most useful technique. Because, if you have the best intentions, there is no reason for this - you are advised to obtain their permission. Put your hands on your hands when treating someone who is present in the body. Energy comes mainly from the hands. This is because energy helps flow directly to them. You may feel more energy flowing, but in reality, you feel resistance. The feeling of energy flow is resistance. If there is no resistance, it simply flows, without actually feeling how the energy flows. Therefore, do not try to feel the energy, believe in the flow.

Remote treatment is less effective than hand treatment. Sometimes this is better, because, according to the subconscious and your instructions, you do not choose where the energy flows, but leave it where it is most needed. But hand care can be more fun because it is more realistic! Both work similarly to each other.

They Need a Pickup

The other person has to accept your healing. Unless the person is unusually (and probably dangerously) open, you won't be able to remotely heal them unless they know and have accepted that you are doing it right now. You can also do it forwards or backwards in time, but again they need to have agreed to it, and it's confusing to arrange to heal someone at a different time.

This is a one-way street. You cannot consciously or unconsciously relate to a person who does not want to be treated or work (for example, contrary to reflective beliefs). This means that you can do this if you want to be very strong and aggressive, but never more useful. As long as you seek revenge and revenge for your attempts to attack your own energy, you are likely to have a mental struggle with a person. The fact that someone lets you touch to heal a physical being is at least accepted. But you can still take care of parts of the body, especially the wound that needs the most treatment. Therefore, trust is very important. If someone does not trust you, it is a waste of time and time. Typically, a stream of soft energy is used to treat non-invasive energy. When the wall is up, nothing flows

Where Does the Energy Come From?

This is the most misunderstood part of energy healing. There are other comments. Some people think that energy comes from outer space and is sent by doctors (Reiki teaches this), while others believe that doctors use their own energy. Both are true. That's right, you use energy, but practically you can produce an infinite amount of energy. They are similar to factories that produce energy and are very efficient, so production costs are low. You can do this as soon as possible, which makes it virtually unlimited for practical purposes. The energy of each person is different, so each doctor has his own energy.

This only applies to the extent that you want to give what you have. Unfortunately, many people who have no experience of healing with energy try to provide the energy that they value most, but they have no energy! They do this automatically because they automatically accept that they need the same energy as others, and they don't like their language or they're used to smelling their own energy, which they don't feel. Therefore, you need to think that you really do not feel and have your infinite power - you feel it, just get used to it. And when you start to get tired, you may feel lost or dead! This is enough to feel healthy.

You do not have much energy that you do not have! You must! People who try to supply energy very quickly lose energy after treatment (give what they do not need) and feel weak. I believe that this interpretation of truth is closer than at least the transfer or use of your energy beliefs. Because he seems to have a unique energy, but in limited cases all the soloists are not so unique and true. You have infinitely large amounts, people who follow my advice and do not try to give away the energy that they value most, can no longer tolerate it.

To do this, you think that you have energy and want to give yourself what you have. This works if you make this intention only once, and then take a break from treatment with or without an attempt. If you set this goal in several sessions in a row, it is set unknowingly, so you don't need to think about it anymore. It is also very useful for this. Provide what you already have as a general rule of life.

How Does the Healing Really Work?

Your energy is your story. You are here (because you were born in accordance with these instructions), where you are now, including how your ancestors came. There have been millions of years of problem solving and adaptive growth. Therefore, energy includes solutions to all the problems that you overcome. If sick, the immune system disappears. After the fight, you now have disease resistance or immunity. Why? Because the immune system has learned a strategy to defeat the disease. The word "strategy" sounds very formal and courageous, but a real strategy is not a set of rules.

To get to the beach from my villa, go left, right, right, right (this is the rule). I did this, but I had to avoid the dog sitting on the road and waiting for traffic jams, etc. The whole story goes from A to B and contains the rules and events that need to be adjusted. If you close your eyes and try to follow Google Maps, you won't have to go there if you overcome obstacles in all directions. This metaphor is exactly how energy healing works. Your energy tells the story of how you deal with the same problem. They teach how to unconsciously overcome their problems.

Of course, this only works if you have solved the problem yourself. Everyone has their own experience, so everyone has something to offer, but it really works if the trustee solves the problem. This is why other therapists are attracted to other people. Sometimes your energy has a big impact on one person and another. They just give you energy for everything your body wants. Sometimes this person needs it because he has found a way to solve the problem. They have no energy to do this. But if they do not understand and do not understand, this will only help temporarily. It will not last long. You feel better for a short time and then return to normal after using the excess energy you just received. In other words, you do not need to search and spend the way to solve the problem with the help of energy.

Therefore, the doctor can greatly help. If you are looking for a cure, it is best to visit many different therapists, as everyone can offer different pieces of the puzzle. More precisely, your energy is not only your energy, but also your story, but you can ignore it. Use it as a story and energy. They melt it and turn it into their own energy if they want. Love food.

Healing Hurts

The pain is painless, healing, pain. If you get injured, pain behind the wound. You are drunk, not sick. I know that something is missing, not theft, and now I need to solve it. Therefore, people avoid healing because healing is painful.

If you are a doctor, some people will be brought to you. These are people who need your energy and who want to be healthy. Some people do not have an opinion in any case, they are people with problems, and you cannot help. Good. You can still be friends. And some people are actively hostile for no apparent reason. These are people who can be treated, but they cannot resist pain. When they are near you, they feel pain and blame you for what you can avoid. I have no idea to help them.)

What You Get in Exchange

When you relate to someone, you also receive energy, especially energy from them. This is good because they have their own infinite energy. This is a one-way street. Maybe their energy is very useful for you or not needed.

Do not try to stop their energy from reaching you. Otherwise, your energy will stop them at the same time.

Therefore, Reiki says that he will heal the person he healed. Reiki says that you are healed because energy passes through you. I think that there is an element in the sense of resuming supplies by accumulating energy reserves and getting fresh energy from the surrounding energy. But in most cases, it is believed that the energy received comes from others. This is because mood changes after treating others.

Receiving Negative Energy from Others

I heard that some people get negative energy from those who are trying to cure. This did not happen to me, and this is because I could not believe what was said, that I did not accept it.

You should not be ready to accept negative energy from others. But if you are afraid not to get negative energy, you need to open it yourself. Fear of something is a strange masochistic way of encouraging desire, or at least that. They usually understand what you are afraid of, or rather understand what you are focusing on (positive or negative). I think the best advice is the best advice when you think you are devouring negative energy from someone or not treat her, or face this fear. If you are afraid of it, it will happen, face it or avoid it.

Some people perform a cleansing ritual after healing to "eliminate" negative energy after healing. This is good, but the idea of not using this energy seems to work well.

Symbols

The symbol is clear. The use of symbols in Reiki is less common under other conditions. In essence, a symbol is similar to a word, a form that is associated with a more complex intention / meaning, so you can only suggest or draw a predetermined symbol for this purpose so that you can offer all the intentions. Display. In the same way, I can say "table" and you will understand what I mean without explaining how it looks. Words contain meaning.

You do not need symbols, but they can be very useful. This is a matter of personal preference. The advantage of getting a predefined character in your form is that you get it with your natural intentions. You intend to accept the intent associated with the symbol and act as you think when you use the symbol. Here's how it works. Once again, this is another starter suitable for beginners. But there is no reason to create your own symbol with the intentions that you have set, or to follow the flow and express intuitive intentions that the energy will do everything possible for the healed person. Different approaches work best for different personalities, so it's up to you.

Intermediate Level

Now get your intermediate care first. Experience in improving treatment has shown the following:

Breath work

Deep, regular breathing is real. This allows most of the energy to come from breathing, which allows you to produce energy faster and more efficiently. Breathing is an area in which this technique has a certain effect that is actually useful for its purpose. Breathing improves healing. Never seen an episode that didn't help

Grounding

Grounding, that is, breathing is especially good when the feet touch the ground. Feel how the energy rises through the earth, inhale, and flow from you into the fire.

Attention to Energy Flow

Passive attention to the flow of energy and / or the energy field works well. When you say that it is a passive intention, you do not need to try it or try to feel it, but knowing that you feel it, it will become smoother when the feeling becomes more realistic than you. This passive, convenient and pleasant attention is the key to a good flow of energy. Secondly, the best way to wander around the mind. Gives worse energy

You can practice self-healing simply by feeling the energy of your fingers, hands, or other parts of the body (or everything else). Passive attention to this part of the body becomes more sensitive and delicate, allowing more energy to flow into this area. After a little practice, you can fill every part of your body with energy.

Love and Intuition

If you evoke a feeling of love or another feeling suitable for this person, the healing effect will increase. Do not force it anymore. Do not worry if this does not come to you naturally. You will already be on the right track. The feelings that people call love are not the same for everyone. This is a comprehensive term that means that although most people do not change their lives, this person considers it important. With a little practice and empathy, you can intuitively see what this person usually needs. Do not leave it alone.

Looping Through the Rainbow

I read it in a book and tried it, and it actually works well. Tracking rainbow colors and representing each color seems to improve the healing effect. Since all colors are associated with energy, and all colors are associated with different chakras, I think you should consider everything that you want to get the full energy spectrum. I usually have bright red, bright orange, bright yellow, herbal green, sky blue, navy blue, purple, dark purple, honey, silver, gold and white.

Structures, Clouds, Bandages

You can do your best. Follow people and try to create a slow energy cloud. They are trying to end medical associations and more. Everything seems to work, and sometimes it's fun to end the session with one or more of these things, giving people extra healing. Of course, not everyone likes structure, so make sure you feel that you fit your style. Technically, he entered into a spell. Design, but based on structural magic (man), non-intuitive magic (woman), but good.

Masculine and Feminine Energies

When recovering, use a combination of gender and gender, like all of us. But in general, men have a lot of masculine energy, women have a lot of feminine energy, and in general there is more energy than a small difference. In fact, you need both for a better treatment session. For example, male energy is much more aggressive. Like a knife or needle that removes problematic energy that leads directly to the wound and causes clogging. The energy of a woman is much more healing, including contributing to the growth and healing of energy wounds.

Too much masculine energy can solve the problem, and then an open wound can damage the aura. This will only cause other problems and prevent the rooting of negative energy. Using too much female energy often helps transfer and restore the body's energy for healing, as it often fails to reach the root of the problem and usually requires the body to do this on its own. It is an absolute miracle that men and women treat the same person at the same time. But by practicing and experiencing, you can develop more different free energies. I found that the left hand facilitates the supply of energy to women, and the right - to men. Who knows! Has the meaning.

Advanced

We are entering this area now. Everything that I have said so far works on the first level of each aura, and even if it bleeds on a different level, it can directly affect other levels. Our bodies are based on the first level and form. It is a physical and tangible form. The next step is a general energy-based atmosphere, such as a cloud of soft energy in which you usually work. But the level continues, switching between form and energy aura. The next level is another level, based on the form, where you can visually (with your inner vision) see the structure or model that the body is trying to match. At this level, you can see the blocks, parasites and implants that cause the aura to interfere with the body. These objects actually exist physically at this energy level.

Cleaning the energy field is often temporary, because at the level of aura 2 there are blocks, parasites or implants. However, without eliminating the cause, it eliminates and heals the effect of Level 1 aura. Now I know that the belief is widespread that all the underlying causes are based on feelings or beliefs. But emotions and beliefs are physical structures in a higher-level mood! They actually exist in the form of higher frequencies. This is the same as the idea that it really exists as reality in this world, but at a higher level. If you know at this level that you can work through intentions and practices, you can do this level yourself.

Implants, Bids and Gags

Implants are metal-like structures. I. They are tough and do not move. I think they were posted by my other people or ghosts, but usually by others. Implants are usually in the form of rolls, needles or chips. I saw a cage full of heads and full belts. In fact, everything that you can think of at the physical level can be passionately introduced into the level 2 aura. Because both levels and some follow the same physical laws.

There are also fabric or leather covers that others can wear. For example, there are contraindications to limbs, such as giraffes in the mouth or throat, so that no one can say anything. The victim is often unable to speak due to such a mistake. These things are determined by the evil intentions of others. As a healing, you don't need to know what you are doing, but you are still doing a certain thing ... to deliver it to people, they don't need to know what they are doing, you are unconscious. This does not mean that you did not do this on purpose. This happens intentionally and unconsciously when something in your subconscious mind is unconsciously more honest with your true intentions (good and bad) than with your conscious / famous self.

This sturdy construction is easy to remove because it does not fight. They just work. To delete, if you are at this physical level, you must delete it in the same way. The second level of aura, in one form, is more sensitive to imagination than this physical level. People use these implants with their imagination, so you can imagine how to get rid of them here. For example, you can imagine and cut yourself with a saw blade. But be careful not to offend anyone. Sometimes they can be reduced only by reduction. Sometimes screws and screws hurt a person, which allows him to rotate sensitively. You should be able to see how to install it, and you can download it in the same way

When you imagine that you are interacting with a second-level aura, you do not need to exaggerate your imagination, imagining that what you do does not bring success. This should actually work. This is another way to present something. This is close to imagination, but you cannot imagine it. When you hit something, it's not just an imagination that it moves, it must move by itself. Another word is required to interact with Level 2 Aura. In the end you will practice. Caution - you are in a strange body! The needle is easily removed, cut into small pieces and carefully removed. Rolls are quite complex, and sometimes they need to be cut into small pieces to remove them without damaging the human body. Apparently, they later recovered and connected.

A chip is fun because it is like a sophisticated technical implant. In fact, I did not believe in it until I saw it myself, and then I didn't understand that another doctor saw it. But relatively easy to remove. They seem to emit unhealthy frequencies that interfere with the mind and body of people.

Parasites

Evil! This evil. They exist as a group of animals at this level, and parasites also exist at this level. They usually sit in energy centers, chakras, consume this energy or sit along the spine. They often find the necessary chips and parasites. I think this is because the parasitic frequency of the chip can attract the parasite or weaken the surrounding body, causing the parasite to take root. What I see is a millipede, very small spiky legs, similar to a head with teeth. In addition, people grow everywhere with paths such as octopus or tree roots.

What I see is a millipede, very small spiky legs, similar to a head with teeth. In addition, people grow everywhere with paths such as octopus or tree roots. If you have sharp legs, you cannot easily remove them. It is easier if you can work with others. When you remove a parasite, you can instruct it to remove the parasite, and when you pull the meat around you, you can imagine how slippery it is to cut. You can also cut and delete files a little, but you run the risk of leaving them behind. If you do not raise your head, it can grow. Exchange is usually possible, but it is a process that requires patience and patience. As I said, it is much easier if you can interact with healing and work together.

Parasites will also share love if they do not receive the negative energy that they eat. Therefore, you can get rid of it by changing your faith and behavior and healing the first steps of the aura with those who support negative thoughts or negative beliefs. But this is a kind of chicken or egg, because parasites cause negative behavior and way of thinking. Therefore, if you ask him to change his faith, you must ask him to reject the parasite. Remove it, cure the first stage of mood and change your negative beliefs, actions and thinking.

The Mind Is the Body and The Body Is the Mind
Everything in your body and in your body, the aura, affects your mind. Their opinion is not only your opinion, but also your opinion about everything. Your faith is not only your faith, but also faith in everything in you. When the parasite dies, the owner feels pain. Technically, this is part of it. When the parasite becomes hungry, the owner wants to feed him. It is the same. Those who have been partially treated are also parasites! If you do not want to get rid of parasites, then the host is at least partially identical. Therefore, you need to learn to distinguish the feelings of other creatures that have their own feelings and feelings. The general trick is that powerful and demanding voices are not real people, but

calm and confident voices that they know tell the truth. It's true

The same as the chip affects the mind of the host. They make programs and do things that they don't need. That is why it is so difficult to change beliefs. Negative behavior is actually good for parts of the body (such as parasites) and not for parts that must exist. In addition, parasites and French fries can be useful in certain periods of life, in times of despair. People often invite them in difficult times of life, because the energy provided by the parasites helps them to strengthen, not feel, ignore the truth and act more actively. No one has the energy to do this. He refused to leave, helping them in a desperate situation when there was no one to turn to them. Or he seduces the owner, tells them that they can help, says that they can do it for a while, and then stops doing it when they depend on him. Sometimes people want parasites. Even if it causes all kinds of problems, it depends on energy. For example, they do not want to find something in their life, their parasitic energy calms. In this case, no one can delete it. They will secretly upset attempts to remove it.

Maybe someone invited the parasite a few years ago and said: "Thank you for what you did for me. That might work. Once a parasite grows with people, it can exist at a young age and in a strange way, like a couple. I have a stubborn parasite that refuses to make every effort to eradicate it, but in the end, I apologize. Broken love!

For all these reasons, a person must actually change his beliefs and act accordingly. This often means acting against your feelings (parasitic feelings, not others). Then you need to suffer from dying parasites. Because it hurts, because it is in him. You must choose and act with your harsh feelings so that a soft and subtle voice whispers the truth. For this reason, energy operations are very useful for quickly redirecting this process. In addition, this parasite is the same as an evil spirit. But on the second level, their aura: On the first level, they are more like ghosts.

Super Complex Stuff

A year ago, I conducted a test in which 20 experienced meditators were recruited to meditate on a symbol to add healing energy to the pond, consuming energy in the pool. Each person treats other people at the same time and can be contacted at any time. All of these are based on symbols programmed with complex spells/complex intentions, including many conditions, including temporary contact, only positive energy can be shared

—in this context, proverbs are contracts, computer programs.)

After some trial and error, I managed to fix the spell! The group reviews were very positive. Many people say how their lives have improved, and they can feel the energy when I participate. I learned a lot from this. Especially when I was looking for a group, I learned a lot about what worked and what did not work for the healing distance of time and distance. Unfortunately, if I did not pay people, they stopped doing it. I am very disappointed because I think that they will continue, but everyone is returning to normal life without money and incentives for this. There is a lesson about how most people really do not want to heal. They want to live their life, as they already do. No problem protecting him! (But I admit that I was disappointed with the experience.)

I present this example as an example of the longest and most likely opportunity for healing, working with energy and magic. But there is another lesson learned from this experience. We are in spiritual law. This was slightly improved before the spell worked. This should be determined in accordance with certain rules. They just can't do anything. In particular, you need to know how this works when creating an existing framework for creating something new and creating something new. If this is intuitive, use methods and structures created by others. This is good, but if you want to do something that has not been done before, or to solve an unsolved problem, create a new structure from the existing structure in the same way

—existing or new homemade of the existing stone.

Chapter 4 Fundamentals of Chakra Balance

You feel "turned off" these days? Are you making silly mistakes at work? Are you sick for the third week in a row? Many things can explain these problematic situations, but the main indicator

here is the imbalance of your chakra system.

First of all, what is a chakra? What are the signs of a damaged chakra? Chakras are the energy center of the whole body.

There are hundreds of different chakras, but there are seven main chakras that are commonly focused on. This colorful energy wheel displays Shushumna Nadi, the central channel of the body. The Chakra along Shushumna Nadi is the center of power where the right channel (Pingala Nadi) and the left channel (Ida nadi) intersect. These energy channels and mental health centers form the so-called "subtle bodies." The subtle body is in a different space from the body and psyche and it has a powerful effect on the body, mind, and the whole system. Any disorder or illness of the body, mind, or soul can cause blockage and imbalance. The goal here is to find harmony. For the people who don't think this is something they can possibly achieve, simply pay attention to the chakras to see what is happening within and find a balance.

If you have lost your balance, consider the food you consumed (experiences, ideas, drinks), current living conditions (big chances, travel,) and the current season (heat, cold, wind, rain, wind, etc.) Each of these factors can have a significant impact on the whole sensitive human system. In the philosophy of yoga and Ayurveda; the chakras play an essential role in understanding the social network, "similar" and "opposite balances" increase. This means that you already have an excessive temperature in your body in the form of anger or an upset stomach and adding more heat to this such as hot weather or spicy foods will allow you to experience excessive heat and excitement. Therefore, when you wake up in the morning, add the opposite temperature such as taking a cold shower or eating fresh fruit in order to feel a balanced mood.

In general, there are five warning signs of damaged chakras. Searching for too much or too little energy in each chakra creates an imbalance. Remember, the goal is harmony. It takes effort to balance the chakras. Here are the general warning signs:

Everything feels 'out of place' You are constantly sick

You find yourself making stupid or silly mistakes
Everything feels and looks 'messy'

Each of these common imbalance's manifests in a particular physical, mental, emotional, and spiritual imbalances in each chakra. Let's take a closer look at how imbalances in each chakra can cause a sense of disharmony in all body systems. As such, we will dedicate an individual to each of the chakras located throughout the body.

Chapter 5 The Root Chakra

he Root Chakra or otherwise known as Muladhara is the most critical and fundamental energy center of our body. It is situated at the base of the spinal column or groin. The Root chakra regulates

energy related to our instinct, survival, and security. When the root chakra is out of balance with trauma, mental problems such as chronic anxiety, psychosomatic oppression, suppression, the flow of life is disrupted. Often our blocked energy centers cause problems in our lasting and personal relationships.

The root chakra is one of the most closed off and limited energy fields in our body. Everyone struggles with the deficiency of the root chakra at a certain point in their lives. If you grew up in an unhealthy environment such as having divorced parents, living in poverty, or exposed to any type of physical or emotional abuse, you may have broken root chakra.

Mending the root chakra requires the act of opening, refining, purging, keeping up, and reinforcing the root chakra in our body. Recuperating the Root Chakra includes the use of specific affirmations like food, yoga practices, sounds, healing crystals, smells, and other holistic medicines in order to restore harmony in the mind-body.

Symptoms of an Unhealthy Root Chakra

The most ideal approach to find out if you need to heal your Root Chakra is to focus on your contemplations, emotions, activities, and physical sensations in the body. Here are a few instructions that must be considered.

For instance, you may be someone that is obsessed with money. You worry that you don't have enough; you have thoughts of disaster around the poor and homeless, and you are too worried to focus on overcoming your financial problems. They are triggered every time someone in your family spends too much or if they have full control over their family's financial situation. Here are some indications that you are exhibiting unfortunate chakras:

You have mistrust towards others (trust issues)

You believe that the only person you can rely on is yourself and you avoid asking others for help

You are a workaholic

You have a problematic relationship with your family You are afraid of losing control

You are aware of threats towards you from other people or your environment

You feel dizzy, anxious, roomy, and unfounded almost all-day You find it hard and scary to be authentic to yourself

You feel disconnected from others and nature

You stop eating when you become depressed or anxious

You have problems with your feet and legs, such as swelling, infections, cramps, circulation disorders

You tend to gain weight around the lower body

Root Chakra Blockage

When people mostly talk about unhealthy root chakra, what they mean is that the chakra is "blocked" or is suffering from a deficiency that limits the flow of energy. However, did you know that your chakra can both too active or inactive? So, what is the difference between a deficient and overactive root chakra? The wrong root chakras can be defined as a passive root chakra and overgrown is defined as aggressive.

Deficient root chakra indicates that you are lifeless, lethargic, passive, clogged, and inward.

Overactive root chakra indicates that you are lively, energetic, reactive, aggressive, outgoing.

If a person has a harmed root chakra, they are progressively powerless to issues. For example, they will feel emotions of tension, doubt, and withdrawal. On the other hand, if you have unnecessary root chakra, you tend to experience emotions of anger, workaholic, greed, and accumulation. The question is, which do you have? It is also possible to fall somewhere in the middle.

What is it like to have a healthy and balanced root chakra? If you have a transparent, secure, and agreeable root chakra, you will initially feel grounded and quiet. You will never again have to deal with the dread of being losing control and you will believe in the intelligence of the divine life. Not only will you trust yourself more, but you will also feel more connected to others and nature. If your root chakra is healthy, it will be easy for you to become be your true self and find the inner peace that was always there. You will be able to connect with it more easily. They will yield to the need to fight, defend, and defend rather than adapt to spills and the flow of life.

How To Heal The Root Chakra

Here are some of the best ways to cure a person's root chakra:

Listen to ethnic music. I recommend the sounds of thunder, Mongolian throat, and didgeridoos (Australian aboriginal instrument).

Set a "LAM" for yourself. This sound corresponds the vibration of the root chakra. Take a stab at drawing letters with sounds "lllllllaaaaaammmmmm." You might also want to listen to binaural beats (a type of music mending treatment) that will actuate and eradicate all chakra by intruding on the sound waves.

Take a walk within nature regularly. Pay attention to the relationship between your feet and the ground.

Introduce yoga into your life; stretch your body with comfortable yoga postures such as; baby poses, forward flexion, mountain poses, squats, and fighters.

Eat root vegetables such as sweet potatoes, carrots, turnips, and other root vegetables.

Practice mindfulness every day for at least 30 minutes at a time. Make it a habit to stop every day and watch your own breath. This simple exercise will help you build more mindfulness.

Use and Meditate with Crystals that utilize the Root Chakra Crystals such as Jasper, Hematite, Smoky Quartz, and Cornelia. My favorite chakra root crystal is black tourmaline.

Peel the root chakra with aromatherapy fragrance. Use oils such as vetiver, patchouli, cloves, sandalwood, black pepper, ginger, and cloves.

Practice grounding exercise; grounding is an act of walking on grass or on the ground barefoot in order to replenish the human energy field.

Wear a totem or a piece of runway jewelry. Wear items related to the awakening of the root chakra.

Sit still and imagine a red ball of light pulsing on your root chakra (groin). Imagine all the turbid energy dissolving when touching a red lightbulb.

Take time every day to sit outside and connect with nature. Watch what happens. Watch the birds, clouds, wind, light, and you feel your connection to it.

Use Affirmations or Mantras. Use spells or affirmations to reprogram your subconscious mind. Examples of affirmations and mantras are: "I am grounded", "I am centered and holistic", "I believe in the wisdom of life", "I have everything I need", "I am confident and safe", "I surrender", "I am strong, stable and peaceful."

Drink herbal tea. Drink powdered tea with chakra roots, herbs like ashwagandha and cloves.

Bathing with soothing water is a powerful method for removing clogged and clogged energy. Or, you can use a bath with mineral salt such as Himalayan rose rock salt.

Check the cause of your fear. Fear arises from your unresolved pain, inner beliefs, and dissatisfaction. Take the time to reflect on the roots of your worries in a diary or with a trusted friend, partner, or therapist.

Train catharsis every day at purification to actively dissolve the blocked root chakra energy. You might want to explore dynamic meditation or actions like jumping, kicking, punching, screaming, or dancing to release your tension.

Chapter 6 The Sacral Chakra

The Sacral or Swadhistan Chakra is the center of our emotional, creative, and sexual energy. The sacral chakra is located three inches below the stomach and above our genitals. It is associated

with an orange color. It regulates energy related to desire, sensuality, and pleasure. When the sacral chakra becomes unbalanced due to traumatic experiences in early and old life, many physical, emotional, psychological, and interpersonal problems begin to arise.

When was the last time you felt sexually desirable, passionate about life, feelings of love or creativity? The vitality that you want to achieve is possible when your sacred chakra is in perfect harmony. People with balanced sacred chakras radiate warmth, joy, and good mood. Unfortunately, many life experiences can cause a blocked sacral chakra. If you have experienced authoritarian education, sexual harassment, toxic relationships, religious teachings, or critical forms of social conditioning that have restricted your flow of vitality, you may have damaged sacral chakra.

Healing the sacral chakra is the act of opening, filtering, purging, supporting and fortifying the sacral chakra in our body. Recuperating the sacral chakra includes the use of several holistic solutions, such as sports therapy, aromatherapy, crystal, and sound, crystal, to restore harmony in the body-mind.

Symptoms of an Unhealthy Sacral Chakra

You are dependent on anything that gives pleasure, such as food, sex, gambling, drugs, work, forced shopping, alcohol, etc. You feel emotionally numb or cold, and it is difficult for you to feel any emotion

You are sexually frigid and have a weak libido that does not exist, or they are too sexually impulsive

You are neurotic and cannot handle spontaneity or insecurity You have reproductive problems such as infertility, impotence or menstrual problems

You are always tired and don't have much energy

You feel disabled and depressed because you express your true feelings and desires, or you are very emotionally reactive

You are emotionally over sensitive or overly insensitive

You have diseases related to your lower back, kidneys or stomach

Sacral Chakra Blockage

Did you know that there are two kinds of chakra that have irregular characteristics? What's more is that Yoga is a great method to conquer a person's body an unblock their vitality. The following are the details of the differences between the two:

When you have a deficiency, you are lifeless, passive, listless, and/or sluggish.

When you have an overactive chakra, you are aggressive, lively, reactive, and friendly.

If the sacral chakra is not active enough, you are more vulnerable to problems such as overly emotional, sexually uninterested, and even feel physical discomfort during sexual activity. Overactive sacral chakras, on the other hand, are susceptible to addiction, sexual addicts, and emotional outbursts.

What are the shapes of a healthy and balanced sacral chakra? If you have transparent, secure, and harmonious sacral chakras, your skin will actually feel better at first. You will no longer fight against guilt or sexual pleasure but respect and enjoy your sacred sexuality in a balanced way. Not only will you enjoy the pleasures of life, but you will also be open to experiencing life even further and increase your desire for it. You will be open emotionally and feel more connected with firm boundaries. You will also get your creative flow back and enjoy the spontaneity of life.

Healing Sacral Chakra

The best way to treat the sacral chakra is:

Open the "frozen" energy channels inside you by perfecting your emotions through catharsis. Try to shout, jump, cry, or other physical forms of purification that trigger emotions.

Check your creative self-expression. This is most suitable for the blockage of your sacral chakra. Choose activities that interest you, such as jewelry making, sculpture, cooking, painting, quilting, and photography! Remember that art requires practice, commitment, and time. Think about what you want to express mentally or emotionally and begin to build, paint, tie, or describe your inner desires.

Check for sexual disorders. Sacred closure without chakras. What beliefs, ideals, and prejudices did you learn in childhood? You can record this by talking talk with a good friend. After identifying your blockages, they can be improved further.

Meditate and use the most suitable crystals for overactive chakra and blocked chakra. Use sacral chakra crystals such as; moonstone, jasper, calcite orange, and carnelian moonstone. My favorite holy chakra crystal is yellow.

Pay attention to your emotional triggers. Emotional triggers can be improved by better adapting to them. For example, when you are angry, slowly relax and take a deep breath. If the blood temperature rises during a specific topic, ask yourself why, and begin to manage your feelings.

Increase your consumption of ginger. Ginger is a warm and irritating herb, ideal for sacral chakras. Use ginger oil, cook more with ginger, or drink more ginger tea.

Explore the sources of addiction. Often, substance abuse is a way to cope with reality and fill the void in your life. Ask your diary or friend or therapist why you rely on something. Ask questions like "Where am I when I'm addicted?" "What do you think of this addiction?" I think you are suffering from a severe addiction. Book with an addiction specialist.

Practice personal care for your body. Accept all body types and other physical discoveries using materials such as meditations and books, and seminars, and reflections. Do not apologize for your appearance but begin to feel your body and its unique needs. Find out which diet plan works best for you and stop eating processed foods. Try to eat foods such as; sweet potatoes, coconuts, apricots, oranges, papaya, almonds, carrots, and mangoes.

Use color therapy to block overactive sacral chakra. The color of the sacral chakra is orange, so add the color of orange through consuming peaches and apricots. You can also put on orange clothes, wrap yourself in orange items, and express yourself with creative oranges.

Imagine a 3-inch neon orange light beating or spinning under your stomach. Feel how the orange energy of the ball dissolves all your blockages or the flow of aggressive energy.

Break out of your comfort zone! For example, go see a movie that you have never thought you'd see or go to a place you could not imagine

Explore other creative forms of sexuality with a partner. Explore various forms of creative pleasure in solitude. Ask yourself if you feel any blockages, such as guilt or shame.

Clean the sacral chakra with aromatic oil. Suitable for the absence and obstruction of the overactive sacral chakra. Use oils such as bergamot, ginger, neroli, orange, jasmine, and rosewood. Eliminate clogging with yoga. Yoga is a phenomenal method to conquer your body's blocked vitality barrier.

Speak positively to yourself every day, this will cause reduce the overactive blockage of the sacral chakra. Say words like; "Accept my inner desires," "Respect and respect my body", "I abandoned my creative inner feelings."

Chapter 7 The Solar plexus

The sunlight-based chakra is the focal point of our will, confidence, and energy. The solar plexus chakra is located about 5 inches above the center of the diaphragm and is associated with yellow and fiery

elements. This chakra regulates the energy associated with vitality, intentions, behavior, and personality. The solar plexus chakra shines as bright as the balanced sun, which is why it is known as the energy center of the "brilliant stone." Have you ever experienced confidence, independence, and internal motivation in your life? This is easily achievable when the sun powered plexus chakra works in congruity with our inner selves under optimal conditions.

However, life is full of traumatic experiences and thoughts that can cause blockage, suppression, or stagnation of the solar plexus chakra. If you experienced a strict upbringing, bullying or have been subjected to sexual, mental, physical and emotional abuse as a child you may need to focus on your solar plexus.

Healing the sun-oriented plexus chakra requires you to open and sanitize the sunlight-based plexus chakra in our body. The treatment of the solar plexus chakra involves restoring the harmony of the body and mind with a range of solutions such as; emotional therapy, aromatherapy, exercise, sound, and exercise.

Symptoms of an Unhealthy Solar Plexus

The best way to determine if your solar plexus chakra needs to be treated is to focus on the physical feelings of your body. Here are a few things to look out for:

You generally feel worn out and apathetic You have problems with overeating

You tend to be easily manipulated by others for their own gain You tend to harass or be aggressive to others

You have a lack of trust in society You seek validation from other people You have low self-esteem

Your body temperature is either freezing or really hot You tend to easily get addicted to things

You struggle with setting boundaries with people

You have stomach related issue, for example; diabetes, IBS, hypoglycemia, or ulcers

You often suffer from gas, abdominal pain, or constipation. You are overweight around the abdomen

Solar Plexus Blockage

Solar plexus chakra can either be at deficient levels or overactive levels. When a person has an inadequate solar plexus, they feel sluggish, aloof, and low energy. When a person has overactive levels, they are aggressive, lively, reactive, and agitated.

Therefore, inadequate solar plexus chakras are more vulnerable to problems such as fatigue, inferiority. Then again, if you have a chakra with a deficiency of sun-oriented plexus, you will express traits of selfishness and anger.

Healing the Solar Plexus

At this point in the book, we have learned several types of transcendent sunlight that is based plexus chakra therapeutic practices. By participating in it, you will maintain a distance that you set for yourself in order to get back in touch with your dynamic focus. Below are a set of instructions to follow in order to heal your chakra:

Get out of your comfort zone and start exploring the world around you.

Remove people from your live that do not encourage you. During this time of healing, you will need the help of people who can encourage you and not the involvement of unsupportive people who will drag you through the mud. This is entirely dependent upon you to figure out who get to stay in your life and who need to go.

Identify the biggest obstacles in your life. What is something that you are continually battling against? Are you anxious about? Could you repeat that? Frequently, people with blocked sunlight-based plexus chakras keep a close eye on contributing to more battles and obstacles.

Eat more nourishing foods. Incorporate whole grains such as oats and rye which are very effective for healing. Make an effort to include supplementary vegetables in your eating routine such as lentils, chickpeas, and beans. Make sure to incorporate flavors like turmeric, ginger, cumin, and cinnamon as these flavors help warm the body. In addition, include foods that are grown from the ground like capsicums, lemons, pineapple, bananas, and corn.

Spend more time out in the sun. The main solution to recovering your solar plexus chakra is to use the sun itself because the sun is an extremely restorative resource. When a person is suffering from Vitamin D deficiency, they will feel sadness and tiredness. Try talking a brisk morning walk in the daylight, or spend some time watching the sunset.

Find ways to alleviate any annoyances that you feel. When you are able to relieve yourself of any annoyances you will be able to free your sunlight-based plexus altogether. You can relieve yourself of any annoyances and aggression through the use of actions such as working out, crying, punching, kickboxing, or singing.

Utilize refinement herbs. Use herbs that have the ability to clear out the sun-oriented plexus. For example, chamomile, rosemary, lemongrass, marshmallow leaf, and ginger. The best way to consume these herbs is to make tea from it.

Use the following assertions: "I can!", "I will!", "I can make my own choices!" and "I am splendid person!" The more you repeat these assertions to yourself the more they will become your reality. You will be able to reconstruct your personality into one that you deem most suitable.

Develop a good sense of humor. Humor is a great way to make light of dark events in our lives. The darkest times of someone's life can be improved just by using a little bit of humor. Making jokes in light of dark events helps create more freedom in our emotions. The more serious you are, the more effect negative things will have on you.

Make use of the following healing stones: yellow calcite, citrine, golden, tiger's eyes, and topaz.

Be sure to practice your breathing and take a step back to see the bigger picture. In the event that you are struggling to effectively communicate with other individuals, learn to concentrate on your breathing. This will help your body relax and allow you to take a step back to be able to properly deal with the problem at hand. Concentrating on your breathing will help you calm down and be able to look at a situation from an objective perspective.

Clear any obstructions within through the use of yoga. Yoga is a great way to reset your inner self. Try these yoga stances; downward dog, shivasana, and tree pose. Yoga can help you tame and balance all the different chakras and energies inside of you. It will help you be free of stress and be in tune with your physical body.

Visualize the sun-oriented plexus. Start by envisioning a whirling circle of cheerfulness in your stomach. Imagine yourself stroking the globe of light and dissolve any blockages within yourself.

Flush out any overactive chakras through the use of essential oils. Use oils such as dark pepper, cinnamon, rosemary, cypress, clove, and sandalwood. You can put these oils into diffuser or rub them all over your body.

Chapter 8 The Heart Chakra

The chakra of benevolence, or Anahata, is the center of love and balance. Heart chakra is found in the middle of a person's chest in the ribcage area. This chakra is associated with art and the finer

aspects of life. This chakra is responsible for a person's self-esteem, self- acknowledgment, genuine love, empathy, and receptiveness of others.

The heart chakra over the last many years has been recognized as the energy of adoration, solidarity, and balance. Do you recall another other time where you felt open, liberal, responsive, tolerating, and excusing to other individuals? This should nearly be possible if your heart chakra was balanced and in good physical shape. However, if you are familiar with loneliness, isolation, resentment, fear or hatred, you are possibly inflicted with a blocked spirit chakra.

Compassion chakra responsible for clearing, opening, supporting, and purging the center point chakra in our bodies. Center chakra's medicinal qualities include a few producing life-powers into a person's body and brain.

Here are the qualities for a person who is suffering from lack of heart and compassionate chakra:

You feel separated from the network around you

You judge others from a distance in order to avoid mingling with other individuals

You feel deprived in human connections You are afraid of life

You acquire your self-esteem through other people and not through yourself

You continuously feel anger towards other individuals/life You always feel like there is social tension

You frequently feel envious of other individuals

You are consistently replaying or remembering feelings of hurt You always feel an overwhelming sense of dread

You fight for other people to give you affection

You are constantly suspicious and doubting of other individuals You have health issues with your heart, lungs or chest state, for example; asthma or high blood pressure.

Symptoms of an Unhealthy Heart Chakra
Did you know that there are two types of chakra that are opposite in character? While an uneven personality

chakra is characterized as "numb," an uneven soul chakra is characterized as forceful or hyper. Here is a breakdown of the differences between the two:

Deficient: You are inert, drowsy, inactive, and hindered (not enough vitality is streaming in).

Overactive: You are energetic, upset, responsive, and forceful (too much energy flows in).

Therefore, if you have an inadequate amount of soul and personality chakra, you will be subject to additional issues such as; social uneasiness, detachment, and self-basic considerations. On the other hand, if you have too much compassion chakra, you will be subject to tenacity and repressing feelings of love.

What you are able to balance your heart chakra, you will initially feel responsive. You feel as if you will never again battle with disengagement, dread, and harshness. However, you will showcase a large amount of kindness to other people. You will fight through your own weaknesses in order to acknowledge the love you have for yourself and others. Therefore, your friendships will grow, and you will prevent others from harm even if they have hurt you in the past.

How to Heal your Heart Chakra

As traditional form of balancing your center chakra, you will practice a technique called 'Woodland bathing'. 'Woodland bathing' is a technique that originated in Japan and was known as 'Shinrin Yoku'. It has numerous advantages that has been proven through many experiments. Here is how you can practice woodland bathing:

If you don't live close to a forest or the woods, don't stress out about it. Simply take a trip to the nearest forest, national park, or any region with a lot of greenery. If you live in a big city that has very limited nature, visit your nearest park or simply surround your home with indoor plants and greenery.

Begin to practice mindfulness and analyze your thoughts when surrounded by nature. If your benevolence chakra feels clogged, begin to reflect in oneself.

Find a private area to sit and be mindful in. Begin to analyze the times in your life where you are allowing different people to affect you. Think of the times where you have said "yes" to requests when really what you wanted to say "no". Whom in your life requires a lot of time and effort from you? Prepare yourself to say "no" during the times where you want to say it.

Treat yourself with herbs. Use herbs such as roses, bounces, astragalus, hawthorn, angelica, and blessed basil to clear the love chakra. One of the best ways to use herbs is to drink them in a tea. To heal your center point chakra, I suggest Buddha Teas' serene and the natural soul Chakra Tea.

Sympathize with yourself and others by asking "How would I feel if I were in their shoes?" This technique is able to clear any blockages that is capable of having the mind make up rash judgments about other individuals. These judgments are often unforgiving, and cold. For example, if an unpleasant person is being impolite to you, ask yourself, "What has happened in their life to make them the way they are now?" Or you can dig even deeper and ask, "What happened in that person's childhood that shocked them so much that they don't have the ability to connect with others?"

Connect with other people more. People are well-known animals that need socialization in order to maintain the harmony within themselves. Acts of physical socialization like hugging or cuddling opens up a person's energy. Hang out with your friends and family more. In the situation where you are not close enough to an individual to hug or have physical contact with them, you may ask if they are comfortable in holding your hand in order to exchange energy.

Show our feelings instead of hiding them. One of the worst types of savagery within human nature is the one where we avoid feeling our own feelings. Our feelings were not made to be controlled or locked away. Instead, they are the innate nature of mankind. Open up your heart and allow yourself to encounter your emotions.

Grow our love for ourselves and others. We deny love for ourselves and other people as a form of protection. Not allowing ourselves to receive love means that we cannot lose it. Denying love or compliments is a way to unbalance your chakra, instead, test the love that you receive with your thoughts.

Consider healing with the healing stones. Be grateful.

Fix your shadow self. Once our essential chakras are shut down, we are in the act of putting away a part of our miserable vitality into our subliminal minds. Your shadow self is the combination of all aspects of your old and denied character. This includes all contemplations, emotions, propensities, and socially heinous self-image parts that are put away. When you begin to accept those dark parts of yourself, your soul opens a little more.

Focus on accepting parts of yourself that you have tried to hide away and repress.

Sanitize your inside chakra with the use of essential oils. Use oils such as; angelica, marjoram, ylang, neroli, lavender, and rose. You can put these oils into a diffuser, rub them on your wrist, or spray them on articles of clothing.

Carry out an exculpation ritual. Write a loving communication to yourself by requesting absolution and carry out this ritual in a place where you deem it is safe. In the event that you are in an argument with another individual, try a self-structured ritual that incorporates one of the four elements of the world; earth, fire, water, and air.

Keep yourself well-nourished. Introduce the following leafy foods into your eating routine which will help recuperate your soul chakra; celery, kiwi, grapes, spinach, zucchini, kale, peppers, apples, cabbage, pears, chard, avocados, lettuce, peas, and broccoli. Clear out any chakra blockages through the use of yoga. Stretch out and activate your core chakra vitality with yoga postures. For example, camel, cobra, nose, feline, and falcon poses.

Learn about breathing exercises. Since your center chakra is led by the flow of air, learning how to inhale and exhale is fundamental. You can utilize different breathing methods such as; nostril breathing, or organic breathing. Remember, breathing shallowly using your chest does not produce the results that you want. The deeper our breaths are, the more oxygen we present to our cells. The more oxygen that we have within us, the more it can enhance our digestion capacities. In the event that you are sick due to an overactive warmth chakra and begin to feel symptoms of nervousness, low breathing is a compelling practice.

Use positive Affirmations. Affirmations are positive statements about yourself that remind you of the good parts of yourself and help you to feel positive inside. For example, "I am open," "I am who I am," "I love others" "I listen with my heart," "I pardon others and myself" "I care for my internal identity," "I am worthy of adoration," "I cherish myself" test opening every one morning with one of these insistences.

Be sympathetic. Do this by reviewing how to let go of your ego.

Complete something consistently. Stick with things when they become difficult. Removing blockages

Would you say you are a thoughtful individual? Gathering blocked point of convergence chakras allows you to act naturally and with sincerity. In classification to begin your heart, shot liability a little sympathetic all day and speak with others. For instance, your power to give a compliment to somebody or support somebody.

Laugh! Laughing is great medicine and it works with the center chakra. Get back in touch with your inner child and laugh often. While you watch funny cat videos on YouTube.

Yell "YAM!" This positive exclamation matches the fear of the consideration chakra. Try dragging out the letters into sounds, for example, "yyyyyyaaaaammmmmm." You can also prefer to tune in to binaural beats (a way of using music as therapy or treatment) which serves to actuate and clear each and every one of the chakras through sound waves.

Chapter 9 The Throat chakra

Thee throat chakra, or Vishuddha, is the foundation of vitality contained by our bodies. It is associated with truth, correspondence, and being accountable. Situated at the base of the neck, the throat

chakra is related to the color indigo and the bit of ether. This chakra is responsible for vitality and credibility, imagination, and comprehension.

As per the Hindu custom, the throat chakra is the vitality inside in our bodies in control of conveying our individual truth! When tune into the pink throat chakra we are inventive, legitimate, sure, decisive, and certain of communicating our reality to the world.

In any case, when we have a blocked throat chakra we battle with disasters, for example, dread of communicating our verbal forcefulness, musings, untrustworthiness, bashfulness, determination, social uneasiness, deceptive nature, dishonesty, and not have of imagination. In the event that you get a blocked throat chakra, it may have to do with your adolescence. Were you left out of a fortune by your folks or guardians? Did your family make fun of you? Were your considerations, thoughts, and sentiments ignored? On the off chance that you had an inclination that you couldn't transparently share your thoughts and emotions, you developed an unfortunate throat chakra. This handbook will help you start recuperating your blocked throat chakra. Throat chakra restoring involves opening, adjusting, and filtering the throat chakra in our bodies. By and large, throat chakra medicine uses a wide range of all-encompassing therapeutic solutions to align the body, brain, and soul. These cures involve the practices of, for example, recuperating, self-care, self-inquiry, yoga, aromatherapy, dye therapy and countless others.

Symptoms of an Unhealthy Throat Chakra

The technique to identify unhealthy throat chakra regardless of whether you need to unblock your throat chakra is to rediscover intrigue to your emotions, activities, and human environment in your body. Here are specific examples;

You recover it thoroughly to express your feelings in a way You struggle to express your thoughts

You think nobody cares about your sentiments, or …

You probably impulsively express your sentiments to others

You battle karma because o miscommunications in your connections with others

You always feel unnoticed or misunderstood by others You worry you won't be seen by others

You are on edge in discussions You are timid around others

You find it unacceptable to be your true self You are at risk of being stubborn, or ... You battle to share your own thoughts

You have trouble being understood

You repeatedly spend time with people that don't understand you or your feelings

You find it difficult to be genuine with others Your actions don't match your words

You are inflicted with swollen lymph nodes in your neck Your weight fluctuates or remains low

You have hypo or hyperthyroidism You often have ear infections

You often have sinus, throat or high respiratory infections

Throat Chakra Blockage

Did you know that close to each other are two different kinds of chakra? While a blocked throat chakra is manifested as uninvolved or effectively "numb," an unbalanced throat chakra is manifested as forceful or hyper. Here's a breakdown of the difference between the two:

When you throat chakra is blocked, you are tired, drowsy, uninvolved, and hindered (no vitality in you).

When you have an unbalanced throat chakra, you are vivacious, disturbed, responsive, forceful, outwards (too much vitality in you). In this manner, on the off chance that you have a lacking throat chakra, you will not show the following; modesty, vulnerability and mystery. Then again, on the off chance that you get an unbalanced throat chakra you will be obstinate, unfriendly, and have the tendency to be socially oppressive.

What does a nourished and balanced throat chakra look like? When you have a solid and wonderful throat chakra, you will be self- assured in your aptitude to state your opinions and sentiments confidently. You will be open, familiar, and bold to express how you truly feel. Authenticity will be apparent in your connections with others, and you will show your trustworthiness. With a healthy throat chakra, you will have lucidity, trust, euphoria, and bluntness as a final product of a mind that is happy to talk with certainty.

Healing of the Throat Chakra

At this time are the best throat chakra relieving practices which will benefit you if you have a blocked throat chakra;

1. Advantage from having a mantra Useful for: Blockages

Mantras are comprised of repeated phrasing or on the other hand sounds that help you to remember things and bring them to your awareness. Within reach are heaps of ancient mantras, for example, "Om," "Ham-Sa," "Om Mani Padme Hum," "I am," and so on. Some choose mantras related to their preferred spirit or divinity for example, "Shiva," "Kali," "Hecate," "Osiris," "Neptune," and so on. You can also come up with up your very own mantra.

2. Mantra Example "HAM" Useful For: Stronger blockages

This ideal mantra matches the throb of the throat chakra. Hear what you feel into sounds, for example, "hhhhhaaaaaammmmmm." You can also use binaural beats (a professional form of music treatment) which actuates and clears all of the chakras through unpredictable music sound waves.

3. Helpful foods

Useful for: lacking and unbalanced blockages of throat chakra

Introduce the following leafy foods into your eating routine for the throat chakra: blueberries, blackberries, cerulean grapes, currants, kiwifruit, apples, grapefruit, lemons, pears, plums, peaches, figs, and apricots.

4. Firm mending

Useful for: insufficient and undue blockages

Sound healing treatment is useful for decontaminating the throat chakra. Instruments, for example, singing dishes, gongs, and tuning forks because of the selective sentiments they transmit. As well as other sound therapeutic treatments.

5. Start journaling your thoughts Useful for: lacking blockages

On the off chance that you are battling with verbalizing your thoughts and emotions, try different things like expressing them in a private diary. Designate time each day to write down how you feel, and don't worry about grammar, for example, language structure or discipline structure. Permit your emotions and sentiments to course energetically through your hand and onto the page.

6. Inhale into your stomach

Useful for: lacking and outrageous blockages

Talking unnecessarily quickly and rashly, or on the other hand not in any manner, are like a secret language that your throat chakra is aware of and it can thus become imbalanced. Inhale seriously into your stomach therefore

that it extends delicately. Concentrate on this sensation and allow it to center your vitality.

7. Control the following herbs

Useful for: inadequate and undue blockages

Use herbs, for example, elm tree leaves, peppermint, fennel, elderberry, Echinacea, clove, spearmint and cinnamon. One of the top propensities to buy herbs is to lift me-up them as tea. For the throat chakra, I propose Buddha Teas' soothing and 100 percent natural Throat Chakra Tea. This tea is injected with the substance of sea green/blue.

8. Grade treatment

Useful for: inadequate and undue blockages

Blue is the color of the throat chakra. Try gazing at the night sky, covered with blue, or encompassed with cobalt and comment on the distinction. One of my favorite types of treatment is painting. On the off chance that you are good at art, building your throat chakra by painting with dark colors as the main shading.

9. Show appreciation for life by saying "thank you"
Useful for: lacking and pointless blockages

Now and again our throat chakras are blocked for the reason that our minds are full of suspicions and let this "thank you" bubble up within you.

10. Consider with the following,

Useful for: insufficient and strong blockages

Use gems as totems that will support you while you heal your throat chakra vitality. Try using, for example, "lapis lazuli, blue kyanite, azurite, larimar, tanzanite, and sea green/blue."

11. Listen carefully

Useful for: unreasonable blockages

If your throat chakra is increasing in levels of vitality, you may battle with overwhelming discussions and overlooking other individuals. This affection may advance you into getting irritated with your companions, relatives, accomplices or associates. To combat this, practice breathing into your mid-region and listening steadily to what the other individual is saying. Survey their group language – now and then an individual's demeanors don't mix with their words. To tell them that you're listening, nod.

12. Laughter and fun used for clearance

Useful for: lacking and an excess of blockages

Purging is a vitality discharging technique which will help you get rid of impurities in your throat chakra. show your disappointment through giggling or shouting. For instance, on the off chance that you have an extraordinary throat chakra blockage, shout into your pillow.

13. Clear obstructions with yoga

Useful for: lacking and unbalanced blockages

Fix your throat chakra by doing yoga stretches, for example, the fish, lion, and dog. You may also prefer to add in words of one syllable while moving your body around tenderly to activate the blood stream.

14. Sing to yourself

Useful for: insufficient and undue blockages

Singing is an appealing sense to delicately begin the throat chakra. On the off chance that you think unsure, sing to by hand gently absent from other people. You force similar like to pay attention to music or keep an eye on a motion picture that causes you to search for to sing.

15. Flush out the throat chakra with significant oils
Useful for: inadequate and outrageous blockages

Use oils, for example, rosemary, frankincense, myrrh, ylang-ylang, clove, neroli, and eucalyptus. From the canister put these oils into a grease up diffuser, rub them on your wrist (in a watered-down mixture), or clothing them in a diffusing pendant.

16. Drink pure water

Useful for: lacking and an overactive amount of blockages

Pure and/or distilled water is critical for your throat chakra wellbeing. In the event that you accept that your stream is debased with contaminants, for example, fluoride and chlorine, purposeful putting resources into a load up with tears channel.

17. Renew your throat chakra representation Useful for: lacking and extraordinary blockages

Envision an agonizing or whirling circle of splendid naval force diverting in your throat chakra region. Think about the circle of sad vitality dissolving out and out blockages or forceful progressions of vitality in you.

18. Enjoy your downtime

Useful for: lacking and extraordinary blockages

As strange as it might appear, use time your downtime to drown out that incessant voice in your head. By enabling your center impact to rise, you will fortify your throat chakra. Yogis constantly lead pledges of quietness to loan a hand them interconnect included wholeheartedly with senior awareness.

19. Using massages and rubs

Useful for: insufficient and superfluous blockages

Neck back rubs are hence quieting and comforting as they improve to reallocate the vitality captured in your neck. Get out a polo neck rub from a rehearsed masseuse, or then again reason an oversee massager, (for example, this one) to manipulate your neck. I guidance warming up a warm pack and applying it to your segment of land before you rub by hand as this will cheer your muscles to unwind.

20.   Learn to say "no" Useful for: lacking blockages

Learning to say "no" can be one of the most effective things that you can do to improve your throat chakra. Often, we feel compelled to do everything that your friends and family want us to do. However, there is a limit in which we cannot be any more productive. At this point, it is important to say "no". While that may cause some displeasure in your interlocutor, it is important to ser clear boundaries both at home and work.

Chapter 10 Third Eye Chakra

The third separation chakra, or Ajna, is the vitality center point contained by our bodies that is in control for instinct, creative mind, thought, and mindfulness. Situated in the point of convergence of the temples directly above the eyes, the third judgment chakra is combined with the color sky blue and the pineal organ contained by the cerebrum. This chakra orders the vitality connected with knowledge and intelligence. The third eyeball chakra is the vitality hub in our mass faithful for instinct, reality, thought, recognition, and showing. As per yogic way of thinking, the third eye is identified with duality which is a catch of recognition that contradicts truth and is designed only by the brain.

On one event the third eye chakra is in agreement with the have a rest of the chakras, it is asserted that a passage towards profound illumination is opened. At the point when our third segregation chakra is vacuum and adjusted, we set up energy with clearness and have furious passionate balance, understanding, instinct and mindfulness.

Then again, when our third eye chakra is blocked or imbalanced, we watch out for to battle with tribulations, for example, distrustfulness, shut mindedness, uneasiness, pessimism, sorrow, and arranged other psychological instabilities and state of mind clutters. In the event that you meditate you power experience a blocked third look at chakra, accept help to your youth. Is it true that you were brought up in a shut disapproved of family? Was illuminated positive about your adolescence, or were you molded to "comply without addressing"? Was your underlying energy condition genuinely steady? Did you guardians or overseers review your bits of knowledge and points of view? If not, you perhaps battle with third gaze at chakra issues as a finish of your youth molding. Try not to stress, this escort will help you start your private single technique for third acumen chakra recuperating. Third judgment chakra medicinal is the experience of purging, opening, and adjusting the third eyeball chakra in our bodies.

Thirdly, take a gander at how chakra therapeutic utilizes a broad range of comprehensive relieving solutions for pass arrangement to the body, brain, and soul. These cures hold onto practices, for example, contemplation, care, paint treatment, reverberation mending, yoga, self-request, fragrant healing, and a great deal of others.

Symptoms of an Unhealthy Third Eye Chakra

The most important signs to consider whether your neediness to experience third eye chakra therapy is to relinquish fixation to your contemplations, activities, sentiments, and crude emotions inside your body. Here are a few secret signs to be on the lookout for:

You are not often surprised or engaged by the things around you You get rid of tuning into your instincts

You are excessively energetic or enthusiastic

You are consumed by the thought of following a "master plan" that will guide the way that you expect things to be done

You are over and over again preoccupied with your thoughts You routinely drift into inattention to pass up on reality

You are unusually fixated on extraordinary "powers" (ability to interpret dreams, clairvoyance, predicting the future and so on.) You are sincerely receptive and deal with chaos effectively You're dependent on material assets which you acknowledge as necessary to accomplish your goals (shopping, connections, status, sustenance, cash, sex, and so on.)

You are overly fixated on attaining social status and economic wellbeing

You don't seem to be too concerned with connecting with your higher self

Your communications with other people are shallow or impersonal

You have trouble relating to people at a personal level

You don't concern yourself with environmental issues or think about the importance of nature

You are obstinate or set in your ways You seem to be overly liberal

You may choose to flaunt material wealth or social status You are seen as egotistical and conceited

You may experience headaches and other physical discomfort on a regular basis

You seem to "tune out" at times

You're far more concerned about getting the results you want You need center and definitiveness

You might suffer from blurry vision and sinus infections You experience daydreams or drifting away

Third Eye Chakra Blockage

Third eye chakra blockage generally makes you feel as if you are "out of tune" with yourself and the world around you. It is like you are aware of everything that is going around you, but you can't really make heads or tails of what's happening. For example, you are in a meeting, you hear what everyone is saying, you actually understand every word that is uttered, yet you can't really make sense of what the meeting is about. By the end, you don't have a sense of what actually happened. All you know is that you were at that meeting and that various issues were discussed.

Another sign that is illustrates blockage of this chakra is your inability to focus and concentrate especially for longer periods of time. Often, it can be difficult to really sit down and focus on something which you are doing. For instance, you might be watching television but may feel compelled to be on your phone or checking your messages every couple of minutes. If you are reading or attempting to do any type of cognitive tasks, you may find it virtually impossible to actually center your attention for a period exceeding a couple of minutes.

Other folks experience issues with sleep and rest. When this occurs, you may feel tired and very sleepy. However, you may not be able to actually fall asleep once you are in bed. The main culprit behind this inability to sleep is a sense of restlessness and inability to relax. Now, it might the result of anxiety over something in your life. However, a third eye chakra blockage might make it hard for you to just relax and get a good night's sleep.

Lastly, blockages of this chakra are also associated with the inability to establish a good relationship with the circumstances surrounding you. For instance, you might feel that everyone is out to get you at your job. You feel that everyone's got something they want from you or you feel that they are out to get you. The reason for this is that you don't feel entirely comfortable with yourself and the situation you are in. Often, your suspicions and feelings have nothing to do with actually hatred. However, your inability to find a sense of ease may lead you to feel this way. As a result, you won't feel comfortable with yourself and the circumstances you find yourself in.

So, it is important to pay attention to these signs that are being transmitted by your third eye chakra. When you are able to free the blockage, it will be like lifting the veil from your eyes thereby enabling you to see things are clearly as you possibly can. This would certainly be a great way to make your life a lot more interesting and rewarding.

Healing the Third Eye Chakra

This section is dedicated to a collection of practices which are intended to help heal the third eye chakra thereby restoring its functionality and returning the vitality back to your body and life. Here are the practices in no particular order:

1. Open your mind to other points of view and perspectives. Useful for: unreasonable blockages

One of the biggest issues that affect most people with third eye blockages is being unreasonable and even intransigent. This means they are close- minded and have a hard time accepting the viewpoints of others. So, make an effort at being more open-minded and accepting what others have to say and the things they have to offer. It could be that something or someone you dismissed may end up providing you with a wealth of knowledge and guidance.

2. Decalcify your pineal gland

Useful for: physical blockages

Your pineal gland is a minor pea-shaped gland that is located at the top of your head, but deep inside your brain. It is commonly associated with third eye chakra blockages. The pineal gland is in charge of a number of regulatory functions including sleep and mood. Countless ancient societies such as the Tibetan, Egyptian, and Chinese had the idea that the pineal organ is the center for otherworldly awareness. To decalcify your pineal organ, a reduction in fluoride is recommended. This can be done by drinking purified spring water that is free of this chemical.

3. Incorporate mindfulness into your life Useful for: deficient blockages

Mindfulness is that state of being constantly aware of your surroundings at all times. This can provide you with a great sense of joy and pleasure as you being to see how wonderful the world around you really is. So, don't concern yourself too much with what's bring you down. Rather, take the time to enjoy what's going on around you.

4. Venture out into the daylight

Useful for: inadequate and lopsided

Exposure to sunlight in one of the best ways in which you can stimulate the pineal gland. Sunlight activates the functions of the pineal gland in such a way that you won't have to concern yourself with doing any additional exercises. If you spend a great deal of time indoors under artificial lighting, make a point of spending a few minutes outside every day. This will help recharge your body of valuable sunlight.

5. Increase consumption of herbs

Useful for: deficient and extraordinary blockages

Herbs such as lotus, mugwort, rosemary, star anise, passionflower, saffron, jasmine, basil, and lavender are all great at helping develop your third eye.

Many of these herbs can be consumed in the form of herbal tea. This is perhaps the easiest way to do so. Other ways in which you can achieve the desired effect on your body is through incense and essential oils. Scented candles work very well, too.

6. Find out what is limiting your convictions Useful for: unreasonable blockages

Since being unreasonable is one of the main issues with a third eye blockage, it is important for you to figure out what is causing you to become overly unreasonable. Of course, the blockage itself is spurring you to act in this manner. But could there be something else that is also affecting the way you react? For example, could it be that you are somehow afraid of something? Is there a person, or situation, which is causing you a great deal of stress and anxiety? Finding these sources can go a long way into determining what is actually blocking you.

7. Making use of the mantra "OM" Useful for: inadequate blockages

The mantra "OM" is a staple of meditation practice. It is used to help focus the mind on the present and clear up consciousness of the incessant amount of information that comes and goes. Through this practice, the mantra is able to help harmonize the mind and the body in such a way that all chakras (not just the third eye) can begin to open up. This leads the body to open up its natural energetic pathways. It is perhaps the single-most effective meditative practice that you can engage in.

8. Improve overall quality of nutrition in order to free up blockages

Useful for: physical blockages

One of the most common elements that promote blockages is a poor nutrition. Now, it should be said that it is not the nutrition itself that produces the blockages. Rather, it is the intoxication that occurs in the body as a result of a poor nutrition. A diet based on high amounts of sugar, carbs, alcohol and even toxic substances such as narcotics and nicotine can lead to a significant intoxication of the body. This is why reducing the consumption of all of these elements can promoted the body's detoxification. In addition, the consumption of fruits, vegetables, fresh water and tea can help promote the physical liberation of cellular process that, in turn, promote the growth and opening of all chakra centers and not just the third eye.

9. Seek spiritual guidance

Useful for: inadequate and spiritual blockages

Seeking spiritual guidance is a great way of clearing up blockages. If you are connected with your faith, then leaning on it will certainly help you improve your chakras' energy processing. If you are not overly religious, it is a good idea to seek a connection with your spiritual self in the manner that you feel most comfortable.

11. Engage in self-reflection and analysis

Useful for: lacking and a lot of blockages

Self-reflection is a great habit to build as it enhances your mindfulness. Self-reflection essentially consists in asking yourself questions about what you do, what you feel and what you plan to do. You can take on a greater understanding of these ideas by journaling. You can write as much or as little as you want. By having a written record of your ideas, you can get an idea of the progression of your thoughts.

12. Try out stargazing

Useful for: unreasonable blockages

Looking up at the night sky can be a wonderful and exciting task. By staring into the vast expanse of the universe, you can gain a better perspective of the place you occupy in the universe. While this isn't intended to help you feel small, it is intended to help you concentrate your energy on the here and now.

13. Aromatherapy through the use of essential oils
Useful for: blockages resulting from overactivity

The use of essentially oils is a great way to help you relax and calm your nerves especially when you are overactive. My using essential oils, you can help unblock your chakra's energy pathways. Oils such as lavender are ideal to do this. Burning incense is also a great idea.

14. Contemplate yourself as a "third person"

Useful for: insufficient and undue blockages

When attempting Vipassana contemplation, you are embarking on a type of reflection exercise in which you literally see yourself as a third person. This means that you try your best to visualize yourself from the perspective of an outside spectator. The main objective of this is to observe your actions, behaviors and attitudes in such a way that you are not actively involving your feelings. This will help you gain an additional perspective which you may not have at this moment.

15.   Visualize your third eye in action

Useful for: mental and emotional blockages

In this exercise, you will close your eyes and literally visualize a glowing disk in between your eyes. This exercise will help you focus on opening the third eye in such a way that you can bust through whatever blockages there may be. Generally speaking, it is not easy to make this exercise work at first. Over time, you will find that it is not hard, and you can sustain this image for a long time usually lasting several minutes.

16.   Visualize the outcomes you wish to achieve Useful for: inadequate and extraordinary blockages

Visualization is one of the most powerful tools you can use in meditation. It helps to liberate blockages by allowing the power of the mind to open the chakras in such a way that you can harmonize your energy's pathways. When there is a blockage, your energy gets stuck and subsequently stagnates. That is why visualizing the outcomes that you wish to achieve, for any type of situation, helps your mind direct the energy that you seek to channel through the various energy points in the body. For example, if you have an upcoming job interview, you can take the time to visualize the situation playing the outcome in your mind. When you do this, the creative energy of the third eye manifests itself in such a way that you are able to literally create your own reality.

17. Exercises using crystals

Useful for: insufficient and unbalanced blockages

The use of crystals and gems is a common practice in this area. Ideally, you would find a pure stone which you can place in a well-lit area. The sunlight that passes through it will radiate a light which you can absorb by watching it. Examples of these gems and stones include amethyst, shungite, labradorite, sapphire, kyanite, lapis lazuli.

18. Practice a good dose of self-love

Useful for: insufficient and undue blockages

A great way of practicing self-love is through the use of loving affirmations. These affirmations can range from anything such as "I am one with love" or "I am connected to the loving energy of the Earth". Any of these affirmations will help you embrace the loving feeling that comes to you from all corners of the Earth.

19. Regularize your vitality with yoga

Useful for: physical and emotional blockages

Practicing yoga has long been considered to be one of the best exercises to balance out both physical and emotional blockages. You can engage in this practice as much as you like but keeping in mind that you can get the most out of it by practicing it on a regular basis.

20. Staring at fire

Useful for: inadequate and an excess of blockages

Staring at a fire is known as Trataka in Hatha Yoga. This technique is intended to help you visualize the matter that is contained within fire. As such, you will be able to imbibe the healing energy of light and warmth. Also, fire's sacred qualities are useful at stimulating all of the body's chakra energy centers and not just one or two individual ones. Best of all, you can carry out this exercise with a scented candle or in front of a roaring fire in a peaceful and serene area.

Chapter 11 The Crown Chakra

The crown chakra, or sahasrara, is the vitality center contained within our bodies. It is liable for mindfulness, thought, shrewdness, and our bond to the Divine. Situated at the top part of the head, the

crown chakra is linked with the influence purple light and the pituitary gland inside the brain. This chakra helps to transform the energy of consciousness. The Crown Chakra, also commonly known as Sahasrara in Sanskrit. This energy center is considered to be the "thousand-petaled" blooms at the excellence of our control and is emblematically depicted as a lotus flower.

This sacred energy core is the seat of cosmic consciousness that all and every one of us carries. As the seat of divine awareness, the crown chakra connects us to the eternal. In Tantric philosophy, the crown chakra, when in balance gives and receives the energy of consciousness. In other words, it is the connection that we have, as humans, between the restricted and infinite. What does our crown chakra express? How can you be aware of what it's like when it is healthy and open? As soon as our crown chakra is balanced, we can become aware of the various signs that indicate we are at one with our Higher Self. That means that we are in touch with the more sensitive aspects of our being. On the contrary, symptoms of a blocked crown chakra include depression, a feel of disaffection or fleeing from life, and need of empathy.

A blocked crown chakra tends to be the outcome of living in highly stressful environments, fast-paced lifestyles, and dealing with trauma such as those experience from early childhood. But overall, having a blocked crown chakra is the result of neglecting our spiritual self. While this doesn't necessarily mean embracing an austere and religious lifestyle, it does imply that we do not pay the same attention that we would normally to our spiritual needs.

The crown chakra is the gateway to the soul. As such, we need to be aware of the manifestations that our soul has on us. These manifestations can some in a number of ways. Mainly, our sensitivities to the world become more prominent. For instance, you might become more empathetic to the needs or others or feel compelled to take part in charitable actions which can lead to alleviate the suffering of others.

Symptoms of Unhealthy of the Crown Chakra

As we with other chakras, there are telltale signs that indicate a blocked chakra. While there are general manifestations across the board, the fact of the matter is that some symptoms become more pronounced as compared to others. So, here is a list of symptoms to watch out for when it comes to a blocked crown chakra.

Apathy

Lack of sensitivity and compassion towards others Excessive selfishness

Insomnia

Nightmares / night terrors Boredom with life

Feeling of disaffection from others Narrow-mindedness / dogmatism Existential depression

Spiritual disconnection

Rigid and close-minded self-identity Greed and materialism

Lack of purpose and direction Mental fog / confusion Loneliness

Chronic fatigue

Headaches / migraines Light sensitivity

Mental illnesses that include delusions (e.g. Schizophrenia)

While there is no conclusive literature, there have been some links to neurological diseases that suggest that a blocked crown chakra can exacerbate mental illness. As such, it is an often-overlook cause.

A deficient or overactive Crown Chakra

An overactive chakra generally tends to lead the individual to have attitudes that seem exaggerated when compared to the "normal" behavior or regular folks. This behavior can be identified as people who tend to overthink everything, that is, they cannot seem to stop thinking about the problems and situations that may be hidden in everything. They are also overly concerned that everyone around them has a hidden agenda. As a result, they are constantly looking over their shoulder waiting to see when the next attack will come.

Overactivity isn't nearly as common as a blockage, though overactivity is a type of blockage. Nevertheless, when a person has an overactive chakra, it can be rather difficult for them to make the most of their cognitive abilities. This can be seen in people who have trouble concentrating or may display signs of hyperactivity. These folks may not be able to concentrate on a single action or activity while attempting to carry out multiple actions at the same time. This is attitude is hardly conducive to a productive lifestyle.

People who manifest an overactive crown chakra may also have an active imagination. However, this imagination can go overboard at times and even lead to delusions. If this were to be the case, it could be the sign for the onset of some type of mental illness. This is the reason why delusions and hallucinations may be associated with an overactive crown chakra. When this occurs, meditation is the best way in which the individual can harness the power of their "visions" in such a way that they don't torment themselves, but rather, they can find a creative outlet for such feelings.

Healing the Crown Chakra

1. Meditate, meditate, and meditate

Meditation is the best way to restore crown chakra functioning. In short, this meditation ought to be focused at connecting the crown chakra with the violet light that comes from the center of the universe. This light feeds the chakra and allows it to blossom. As a result, the chakra begins to open thereby allowing the individual to connect with their higher being. Also, visualization is useful to connect the chakra with the outcomes that the person wishes to achieve. Again, connect to the light while imagining positive outcomes enables the Higher Self to emerge and connect with waking consciousness.

2.   Conscious shift in mindset

The old philosophical truism that we are what we think rings very true. As a result, it is important to begin replacing negative and unproductive thoughts with positive and creative ones. To do this, all you need to do is tell yourself that you are whatever you want to be. For instance, if you are looking to lose weight, you must begin by replacing thoughts of "I look fat" to thoughts "I am slimming down". If you are looking to be successful in your chosen profession, then you need to begin by telling yourself that you will achieve your goals and dreams. If you constantly tell yourself that you have bad luck and that nothing does right for you, then these negative thoughts permeate your consciousness. Consequently, the crown chakra gets clogged up with negative thoughts. When you shift mindset, you allow the positive energy to flow through your unconscious mind and eventually break through to your conscious mind.

3.   Working with your energy

Energy management is crucial. This includes all types of exercises which can help the free flow of energy throughout the various centers of your body. This many include both mental and physical exercise. Of course, it should be noted that physical exercise is always a great idea to help you get the most out of the physical energy that your body is able to produce. Examples of activities which you can do to improve your energy as qigong, massage, gong, yoga, reiki, acupressure, acupuncture, among others.

4. Educate yourself

The pursuit of intellectual endeavors is algo a good way of helping the crown chakra get into high gear. Intellectual abilities are important because they help the mind develop its abilities in such a way that the individual is able to further their understanding of the world around them. In such cases, reading about any number of topics, watching educational videos, or even taking a class are great ways in which the mind can open up to new information and new challenges. Since the mind acts like any other muscle in the body, the more that it is exercises the stronger it will get. As the crown chakra opens up, you will find that you become "more intelligent" though that intelligence that you have uncovered is mostly the product of a clear chakra as opposed to increased cognitive abilities.

5. "Cleanliness is next to Godliness"

Simplify your surroundings. While this doesn't mean becoming a minimalist overnight, it does mean that reducing clutter around you will help you improve the overall amount of disorder in your life. When you are able to do this, you will find that your mind becomes free to explore the world around it. Perhaps having a tidier workspace will enable you to focus better on your tasks. As a result, you will become more productive and more adept at getting work down under various situations.

6. Use the "OM" mantra.

The "OM" mantra is a powerful too. This channel matches the pulsation of the crown chakra. The effect of "OM" on the brain is similar to that of binaural beats. The effect it has on brainwave patterns is rather similar. So, it can be inferred that the vibration produced by this sound will enable the individual to get the same benefits without having to resort to the equipment and sounds needed to produce the effects of binaural beats.

7. Explore the benefits of herbal medicine

When you suffer from physical ailments (so long as they are not serious diseases) it is best to explore plant-based medicine as an alternative. The reasoning behind this is that natural or herbal medicine helps the body process vitamins and minerals that are needed in order to help the body produce the elements it needs to repair itself. In this way, you can also achieve a healthy mind-body balance derived from your ability to make the most of your ability to choose healthy ingredients to feed your body. So, do take the time to explore the power to herbs when you are suffering from ailments such as a cold, flu, fatigue, or any other type of condition that doesn't require a major medical intervention.

8. Firmly commit to your personal spiritual practice

A personal spiritual practice can differ from person to person. The fact of the matter is that there is no right or wrong way to go about it. We all have different types of activities in which we engage. Some of us a more dedicated to following the guidelines that are established by a specific religion while others are more dedicated to the teachings of a given school of philosophical thought. The truth is that it doesn't matter what type of approach you take. The main point is to ensure that you are aware of what you need to do in order to help you achieve a direct connection with your Higher Self.

That is where meditation and contemplation help connect your conscious mind with your Higher Self. At first, you may simply try to communicate without much of a noticeable difference. Over time, you will notice that your perception of the world around you will begin to change. So, make the time to dedicate your attention to your spiritual practice. It will definitely help you clear any blockages in your crown chakra.

9. Acknowledge the power of prayer

Prayer doesn't have to be religious. You can pray to the higher power in which you believe in, whether that be your Spirit Guides, Ancestors, God/Goddess, Universe, Life, Spirit, or Soul. Prayer is about connecting to the more subtle nature of the universe. The power of prayer is undeniable as it provides a great deal of health benefits. It can also help you to focus on your more subtle energies that flow from yourself to the expanse of the universe.

10. The power of crystals and gems

In earlier sections, we have talked about the importance of gems and crystals. They can help to hone energies into a single spot. The most effective way is to surround yourself with them much in the same manner you would with essential oils and flowers. At the end of the day, this combination will help you focus your energies and concentration on the tasks you need to accomplish.

11. Be approachable to guidance

By being approachable to guidance you are not submitting your will to the teachings and direction of others. What you are going is opening your mind so that you are willing to become more receptive to the teachings and guidance that others, basically any person, can offer you. As a result, you will become more open-minded in such a way that you can take advantage of the various ways in which knowledge can come to you.

When you are approachable, you won't dismiss other perspectives and new ideas simply because they are not the same as yours. You will learn to take everything with a grain of salt while also making the most of your own ideas. When you are able to mesh new ideas with your own, you will begin to grow as a person in such a way that you can achieve a greater understanding of the world around.

12. Positive affirmations

Positive affirmations are related with the universal concept pertaining to the power of word. When you make a declaration, you are letting it be known to the universe that something will happen. For example, when you declare that you are free of all mental bondage, you open up your mind to become liberated of all negative conditioning. Likewise, when you make the most of your understanding of the world around you, you can begin to make sense of how powerful you really are. That is why you need to be careful with the way you express yourself since negative affirmations can work just as well as positive ones.

13. Perform a crown chakra visualization

For this exercise, visualizing your charka as a spinning disk sitting atop your head works very well. This exercise allows you to literally open your mind. As you gain more proficiency with this exercise, you will be able to make the most of your talents by giving your chakra the exercise it needs.

14. Beneficial herbs

Use herbs such a lavender, holy basil, gotu kola, and lotus. As we have discussed earlier, you can consume these herbs by means of an infusion tea, essential oils or even incense. The scent of these herbs stimulates the chakra while allowing your consciousness to become clearer and unimpeded. Also, consuming these herbs in a tea helps your body to absorb the nutrients in a natural and healthy manner.

15. Wear the color violet

The color that is associated with the crown chakra is violet. So, wearing clothing or accessories that contain this color can be helpful in aiding your chakra absorb the energy that is emitted from the center of the universe. In a manner of speaking, it is a way in which you can become more receptive to this type of movement.

Chapter 12 Benefits of Chakra Balance

Once you have put into practice the guidelines which we have outlined in this book, you can look forward to achieving balance among your entire chakra system. As you begin to achieve this

balance you will find that it is much easier to reap the benefits of a healthy flow of energy throughout your body.

As, here are the most important signs which you can identify as you begin to feel healthier, more in balance and in tune with your entire chakra system:

1.   Chakra balance renews overall physical health and wellbeing

Barring any serious physical diseases, most ailments tend to go away when the chakra system falls back into line. The benefits range from a number of minor ailments such as headaches, physical discomfort and digestive distress. A vast majority of folks indicate that many chronic conditions such as fatigue and even weight gain reduce as a result of chakra balancing. Also, conditions such as diabetes, thyroid and hormonal imbalances are noticeably more manageable. So, the physical health benefits are definitely evident when the entire chakra system enters into a state of balance.

2. Chakra balance promotes spiritual and emotional wellness

Balanced chakras tend to complete rejuvenate a person's spiritual wellbeing. Much of this is due to the release of blockages that may be the result of trauma stemming from childhood incidents or the accumulation of stress that occurs over a large period of time. In reality, achieving emotional and spiritual wellness is not nearly as hard as might be considered. Through meditation, visualization and the use of the various techniques highlighted throughout this book, you can ensure that your chakras will slowly, but surely, all fall back into line. So, in addition to physical wellbeing, emotional conditions such as anxiety and depression all have a noticeable improvement over the long run.

3. Chakra balance promotes the release of negative energy stored in the body

The clearing of blockages leads to two things in the individual. The first, is the release of negative energy that is stuck in one, or various, chakra centers. This energy can come from any number of sources but may not find a natural release point. When the chakra system is balanced, the negative energy that enters the body flows through the various centers and exits accordingly. However, when there are blockages, the negative energy has nowhere to go. This is what leads to the overall accumulation of negative energy. In the end, the person feels drained, mentally distraught and emotionally frayed. The second thing that happens when balance is achieved is the flow of positive energy. As such, there is a balance as positive energy cancels out the negative kind. This promotes health, wellbeing and an overall sensation of wellness throughout the body. Mentally, this leads to sharper faculties and better performance in various aspects of life.

4. Chakra balance leads to a greater feeling of happiness

Given the fact that happiness is a relative term, we are referring to a feeling of fulfillment and joy in your life. Happiness is seen as the ability to achieve whatever it is that you wish to accomplish while enabling yourself to enjoy the fruits of your labor. In this manner, you are able to make the most of your time and efforts by leading yourself down a path in which you are surrounded by satisfaction as you transit from one productive stage to another. As you begin to accumulate success and make progress in life, you can then feel a sense of relief and enjoyment at the circumstances in your life. Eventually, you can trade negative feelings pertaining to the situation that you find yourself for a more positive outlook on life. This is especially true when you find yourself in a negatively charged environment such as a bad job or relationship.

5. Chakra balance allows you to connect with your Higher Self

The Higher Self is your soul, essence, spirit, or whatever you may call it. This essence is your connection to the vital core of the universe. Also, it is the way in which you are able to link with the vast expanse of the universe in a type of collective consciousness that most religions refer to as "God". This relationship is fostered regardless of faith as all faiths seek the same close relationship to the divine deity that it worships. As a result of chakra balance, you are able to achieve this closeness insofar as you are able to communicate appropriately, be it through prayer, sacrifice or any other means that you feel adequate such as meditation. In this regard, connecting to your Higher Self is the byproduct of raising your conscious awareness of yourself through practices such as mindfulness.

6. Chakra balance is beneficial in transforming your weaknesses into strengths

Considering that chakra balance involves emotional health and equilibrium, you are then able to tackle some of the bigger issues that may be surrounding you. For instance, you may be dealing with emotional conditions such as anxiety or depression. In this case, you have the opportunity to take a weakness (e.g. anxiety) and transform into a strength. This occurs when you are able to acknowledge the source of such feelings and then transform them into a context in which you are able to process the source of your feelings. In this event, you can now be proud of having defeated the condition which had you down on your knees. While it is true that some of these conditions never fully go away, that is, you may still feel the onset symptoms from time to time, you will be able to manage them in such as way that you will no longer be prey to a debilitating condition. Moreover, you may be able to help others who are going through the same circumstances as you once did.

7. Chakra balance can help you get a grip on your finances and material wellbeing

Healthy chakra balance may also influence your financial life in a positive manner.

This is due to the fact that your emotional wellbeing can be translated into a renewed lease on life focused on the positive. For example, if your previous state was one of fatigue and negativity which was negatively impacting your performance at work, your newfound energy and drive can lead you to find a practical sense of efficiency in your day to day tasks. This will lead you to become more effective at work to the extent that you will now be more productive. This, in turn, may represent a financial gain which may have seemed like nothing more than a dream some time ago. A good example of this can be seen in a promotion at work, or the attainment of your targets. As a result, you will be able to make the most of your time and efforts by focusing on what really matters. All of that negative energy which was dragging you down will now be nothing more than a forgotten memory. So, it certainly pays to work on developing your emotional health through chakra balance as it will definitely have a positive impact on your personal finances.

8. Chakra balance can help you turn your dreams into a reality

A simple example of this is procrastination. When you become a chronic procrastinator, you are falling prey to the cocktail of negative energy that is swirling around your being. As the negative energy vanishes, you can then set out to accomplish what you really want out of life. Ultimately, this may represent going back to school, improving your job skills, learning a language or starting a family. Whatever your plans may be, you will now have the motivation to set out and get it done. This is something which you might not have thought possible just a short while ago.

9.   Chakra balances improves your intuition

Intuition is often seen as some type of superpower in which a person is able to "feel" the truth or reality about something. The fact of the matter is that intuition is a byproduct of that connection with your Higher Self. Your Higher Self is nothing more than that pure essence which is connected to the overall hierarchy of the universe. As your consciousness links up directly with the universal consciousness, you are then able to intuit things that are about to happen, may be happening, or happened without your knowledge. In this regard, you'll be able to "predict" things that will happen, or at the very least, avoid potentially difficult situations. A common example of this can be seen in the way mothers protect their children by intuiting that danger lurks at some point. This is not a superpower, but rather, it is a connect that a concern mother develops with the universe out of the concern for the safety of her child. This is a skill that anyone can develop so long as they achieve chakra balance.

10. Chakra balances helps promote healthy emotional management Emotional instability is general a consequence of pent up negative energy that has nowhere to go in the body. At first, this energy is processed by the body through a series of symptoms such as headaches, physical discomfort (aches and pains) and other conditions such as a weakened immune system. When balance is restored, the body enters a phase in which negative energy can flow out of the body while positive energy transits in the same manner. This gives the impression of emotional balance. However, it is not that there is a presence of balance; the fact is that the overwhelming accumulation of negative energy is gone thereby giving the body the opportunity to process all of these negative conditions.

11. Chakra balances involves full mind-body balance

Perhaps the biggest benefit can be seen in the full mind-body balance that can be achieved through concerted effort in developing chakra balance. In this scenario, the mind and the body synch up in such a way that the body feels what the mind is feeling, and the mind can be used to heal the body. It is really that simple. The body is able to perform up to the level that it was meant to be while the mind serves as the main processing control unit for the entire being.

12. Improved sense of empowerment

When chakra balance is achieved, a sense of empowerment is built up in the body. What this means is that the body is able to feel in good health while the mind is focused on what is currently at hand. As a result, the sense of empowerment emerges. This sense of empowerment is essentially the feeling of control that you have over your mind and your body. One of the most common symptoms of chakra imbalance is a sense of powerlessness over the circumstances surrounding the individual. With full chakra balance, it feels as if the individual is now in total control of not only themselves, but the entire universe around them. If you feel that this is nothing more than gobbledygook, then you will surely think twice when you see that empowerment is entirely possible. You will develop a sense of being the master of your destiny even when it seems like you are not.

Chapter 13 Radiate Positive Energy

Very moment of our lives is an opportunity to immerse ourselves in positive energy. Even when we sleep, we are putting ourselves into a position to receive positive energy from some corner of the

universe. Believe it or not, positive energy travels through the universe just as negative energy does. In this manner, we, as humans, absorb energy on a constant basis.

As we pointed out earlier, when you achieve chakra balance, you are able to take both positive and negative energy and let it flow through its natural causeway. In the end, you are able to balance out your feelings and emotions to a degree in which they will no longer hinder the body. Moreover, this free flow of energy will enable you to feel more at ease with yourself and the universe around you.

Still, for all the negative energy that we receive on a daily basis, we are perfectly capable of becoming a source of positive energy for all of those around us. When you become a center for positive energy, everything around you begins to morph into a more positive environment.

This can lead you to achieve your goals while helping others to achieve a better emotional, physical and spiritual condition. Ultimately, the only thing you are left with is a sense of happiness and fulfillment as you have been able to help others around you feel better.

As such, there are 50 ways in which you can become an agent for change and a source of positive energy.

50 Ways to radiate positive energy

1. Blast out a smile!

Studies have demonstrated that smiling is the only gesture that is universal across all cultures. This means that a smile is a smile in any part of the world. Moreover, it is contagious. A smile will almost always be meet with another smile. So, blast out a smile as often as you can. That way, you can get off on the right foot every time you meet someone.

2. A phone call can go a long way

Phone calls may be a thing of the past… well, maybe not so much. Still, phone calls aren't as common as they used to be. So, a well-placed phone call such as on a birthday, anniversary, or any other special occasion can lead to a pleasant reaction in someone special.

3.   FORGIVE!

Forgiveness is one of the most overlooked reactions we can have. When you forgive, not only does your body actually let go of negative energy, but you are releasing positive energy to the source of your frustration. If you blame yourself for something which happened, then maybe it's time you forgave yourself.

4.   Get into the habit of complimenting

Complimenting for the sake of complimenting is not the idea here. The main idea is to give well-placed compliments when they are earned. For example, when someone is looking their best especially after going through a tough spell is a good idea.

5.   Be civil on the road

All too often we find ourselves duking it out in traffic on a regular basis. There are careless, inconsiderate and rude drivers. And yes, we tend to lose our cool and fight back when need be. However, try your best to be courteous. Give someone a chance to cut in when they are attempting to make a lane change and say thank you when someone gives you a chance. It could certainly make a difference in someone's day.

6. Give small tokens of appreciation

There are times when you can't do much to express your gratitude when someone does you a favor. Sure, you can always say "thank you", but that's often not enough. So, small tokens of appreciation can go a long way to ensuring that your helpful friends and colleagues feel that you truly appreciate what they have done for you

7. Give encouragement

This is one of the most powerful things that you can do. If you see someone who needs a word of encouragement, do it! It doesn't matter if they are a stranger. They will surely pay it forward later.

8. Positive notes

Leaving positive notes lying around is a great way to help you stay on the right side of the ball. Motivational phrases that have a special connection to you work best. Also, inspirational pictures and paintings will help you get through long days.

9. Tip it!

Tipping for service isn't a custom in all parts of the world. Yet, a server will appreciate it if you leave them a tip for their kind attention. Often, they will appreciate the gesture and can brighten up their day.

10. Spread the wealth

By this we mean sharing your good fortune with others. No, this doesn't mean splattering your social media accounts with pictures of your good fortunes. It means that you can take the time to share your good fortunes with those who are needy. For example, you can give to charity or support causes you believe in.

11. Be mindful of the environment

What could be more positive than helping the environment? You can do your bit to help Mother Earth recover from pollution cause by humans. Recycling is a great place to start while ensuring that you do your part by conserving energy, water and trees. Plant a tree if you can. You can watch it grow over time.

12. Keep in touch

Social relationships are a great way of spreading positive energy. Often, all you need is to say hello in order to make someone's day. By being kind and sociable, those around you will feel that you care about them. This is a great way to boost their overall feelings of positivity.

13. Compliment a stranger

When you give kind words to random people such as saying nice things about their dog or thanking them for holding the door, you help spread good will and positive energy. Even something as small as saying "good morning" or "have a nice day" can go a long way.

14. Set goals for yourself

When you set goals for yourself, you are making declarations and statements of what you plan to achieve. As a result, you are not thinking with a limited mindset. Rather, you are thinking with an expanded mindset that is intended to help you make the most of your ideas and aims.

15. Use positive affirmations

Rephrasing everything in life, even problems, in positive language can go a long way toward helping you make the most of your situations. For example, if you are short on cash, replace "I don't have any money" for "where can I get more money?" In essence, you are shifting from a limited mindset to a growth mindset.

16. Donate to a good cause

Often, you don't need to become a billionaire philanthropist to help those in need. You can start by donating unwanted items that are cluttering up your home. You may not need them, but there are others who do.

wish to accomplish, both in your life and the life of others, you will attract the positive and creative energy of the universe. This will lead you to become more powerful than you could have ever imagined.

35. Discover what's inside those around you

How can you "read" people's minds? Ask them! Sit down and talk to those around you. Ask them about their lives and how they feel. Then, make a point of being present when they tell you about themselves. When you listen actively, you create a sense of appreciation in your friends that is unrivaled to anything else you can imagine.

36. Keep an open mind

When you go about your day with an open mind, you won't be thinking about the limiting feelings that come with being close-minded and set in your ways. The end result is a feeling in which you are committed to making sure that others feel you are truly engaged in their needs. So, when someone talks to you about their feelings and ideas, you'll be ready to really listen to them.

37. Live in the moment

When talking about mindfulness, we discussed the importance of living in the here and the now. So, when you do this, you are able to ensure that you are not distracted by things that don't really exist. This allows you to enjoy every second that you spend with your loved ones. Plus, it can help you to let go of those things which may be causing you pain and sorrow.

38. Tend to others in need

Often, we are faced with sick and infirm friends and relatives. In such situations, we can show our appreciation and concern by being in constant touch. This means frequent visits and constant phone calls. You don't necessarily need to be at their bedside 24 hours a day. But by being able to show that you are genuinely concerned for their wellbeing, you can help your loved ones in their recovery from illness.

39. Honor your promises

There is nothing more powerful than a person who is able to honor their word. When you make a promise, you need to make every reasonable effort to keep your word. When you do, you not only boost your personal sense of satisfaction and empowerment, but you are also creating a sense of security and confidence in those who have placed their trust in you. When you build your reputation as a trustworthy person, all of those around you will feel better just by knowing you are around.

40. Sing a song

Yes, singing a song can create a positive environment. It seems a bit childish, but it's true. You don't need to be the next great pop star to sing a song. Still, you can foster a positive environment for those around you when you are able to communicate good vibes through some good tunes. After all, what do you have to lose? Everyone loves to hear a good tune now and then.

41. Set healthy boundaries

It's important to set healthy boundaries around you. Sometimes, it can be challenging to deal with everyone around you especially if the invade your personal space or don't respect your position in life. This is why you need to set your boundaries in a healthy manner. This means that there is a limit to which people cannot cross without making you feel uncomfortable. At that point, you can then make sure that they know they ought to step back.

42. Laugh as much as possible

When you laugh on a regular basis, you release a great deal of positive emotional energy. In this case, you are able to help your body process good emotions while disregarding negative ones. Also, laughter is a sign that you are in a good mood, or at least in a positive one at that moment. Research has also shown that laughter is good at boosting the immune system and helps keep the mind fresh.

43.   Wear bright colors

Colors a definitely power tools. If you were dark, somber tones, they will reflect your overall mood. This includes colors such as black, dark brown and dark blue along with all shares of gray. However, if you choose to wear bright colors, you are automatically signaling that you are in a more positive mood. So, these colors reflect your overall mood. As a result, you won't have to worry about becoming overwhelmed with negative emotion. The colors you wear will help you take a step in the right direction.

44.   Disconnect from electronic devices

Recent research suggests that electronic devices have been a good source of stress and anxiety among people of all ages. In this case, it is a good idea to disconnect from these devices for a while. When you do this, you are able to break free from the constant attention that such devices receive. This is important because freeing yourself from the incessant chirping or messages and notifications can help stabilize your mood and get you to spread the wealth, that is, sharing with others while being in a good mood.

45. Start off your morning with positive affirmations and gratefulness There is nothing worse than starting out your day in a bad mood. After all, don't we all dread Mondays? Indeed, there is nothing worse than getting out of bed only to dread the day that lies ahead. When you are able to transform your attitude from "it's Monday again…" to "thankfully, I have a job", your positive outlook will help offset any pessimistic feelings you may have about the world. Gratefulness is all about focusing on the positive things you have in life and foregoing thoughts that are focused solely on what you do not have. Start off your day in this manner and you will soon find that it is not hard to make a positive change overnight.

46. Focus your energy

One of the worst things that we go as humans is spend our energy on tasks and activities which aren't overly productive. Now, there is nothing wrong with watching TV and surfing the internet. However, these activities become unproductive when you engage in them for the sake of doing so. So, instead of spending your time on activities which you can use to facilitate the achievement of your goals, all you are doing is mindlessly going through the motions of life. Try making a concerted effort to focus your energy and you will find that being ultra-productive is very straightforward.

47. Get the low-down on your friends and family

As we have mentioned earlier, listening closely while others are talking is a great sign of respect and affection. However, remembering what they said is even more powerful. For instance, people tend to drop hints around their birthday or when they are keen on something in particular. It's up to you to pick up on those signs and acknowledge their feelings. When your friends and loved ones see that you are truly paying attention to their needs and wants, they will feel loved, and in turn, give that positive vibe back to you.

48. Effective body language

For all of the positive language which you can use, you can easily derail that by using body language which contradicts everything you have attempted to do. In that case, it's important to make sure that you have coordinated your words with your body language. For example, if you constantly keep your arms crossed and standing in a defensive position, you will instinctively signal to others that you are not exactly in a friendly disposition. When you smile, open your arms and use a welcoming tone of voice, you will find that you won't have trouble relating to others on a personal level.

49. Stop and smell the roses

This is not in the literal sense, but rather, take the time to appreciate the world around you. There are wonders at every turn. You can appreciate the marvels of nature or the incredible diversity in people. You will be amazed at how many wonderful people there are in the world. By the same token, you can take the time to make sense of the bad things around you. That way, you can avoid such circumstances, or make an effort to help those in need.

50. Take care of yourself

The last reflection in this chapter is about yourself. You must make taking care of yourself a priority. This includes a healthy diet, getting enough sleep and doing regular exercise. When you are able to make the most of your efforts to take care of yourself, you are already setting yourself up for wellness. Also, make a point of dealing with stress and negative emotion in a productive manner. At the end of the day, this will help you process your feelings and emotions in a constructive manner.

Conclusion

Life phenomena have two constituents. The first is energy, and the second is biochemical. Energy strengthens and penetrates into matter. Removal from the physique means medical decease. If the

ECG and EEG are not recognizable, scientific demise leads to the destruction of the physique into tiny biochemical elements. We're consistent with two modules: energy and biochemical substances. The vigor that refreshes the body of animals and humans is called life energy. This strength environs each cell with a mini-cable provides a plan for the physique and acts as an intermediate for the stream of data all through the physique. Bioenergy goes beyond the body and generates low-frequency electromagnetic fields (and other sly energy fields, not thus for renowned by science). In a bigger content, bioenergy is a central quality of widespread liveliness.

Bioenergy specialists give information in these areas, as great as the liveliness end through the physique. All that happens in the lions share is reflected in the course of liveliness and secondary versa. After these rivers and fields take back to normal, bioenergy practitioners are supposed to be intelligent to bring back the poise between bioenergy and biochemical mechanism in order to improve their health.

We all know that stories describing abnormal healing reach people. They are passed down from cohort to cohort, in every culture and continentally. When medical research begins, students learn that medicine comes from Greece and that Greece is the main source of medical knowledge. It is no secret that the first medical punishment began in thousands of years in honor of the victories of India, Ancient Egypt, Peru, Mesopotamia, Babylon, India, Mexico, Assyria, and China. It's untrue that we don't have evidence about the initial medication. European archeology, anthropology, and maritime history, as well as reports on traders, missionaries and first adoptive parents, provided valuable information on the complex medicinal processes that were effectively done many years ago. Nowadays new and other medicinal volumes are being interpreted into tongues

Bodily welfare is closely linked to mental well-being, emotive stability, and mystical ethics, and there has always been a common understanding that well-being reflects a person's environment. Most olden and modern medicinal performs base on unaccustomed ideas about death and life are very hard to comprehend because we cast-off priorities, despite documentation and other proof that individuals have done comparable performs all through the past. Affirmative outcomes that indicate mental, physical, and emotive health is understood otherwise dependent on the stage of understanding, conviction systems, and the level of understanding of the essence of the universe. As these performs are incompatible with our worldview, it cannot be explained, based on whatever you studied in school and college, so you decide on the simplest method. These phenomena are very common among those who call themselves "scientists," but their neglect contradicts the norm of methodical methods. Among the early performs known as surrender or, most often, healing through energy transfer.

In the past, ordinary people often severely restricted or prohibited ordination. If you look closely at the culture, you will see that the more structured the societies, the more restrictions there are in this matter, and in many cases, the hands of the community are limited to special groups. For example, in ancient Egypt, only the highest priest and the god of one person or another priest of his choice could heal. Interesting information on how to put your hands on pain relief can be found in Ebers-Papyrus from 1550 BC. In Mesopotamia and Babylon, healing occurred in the provinces of kings and the high priesthood. In ancient Greece, doctors, mathematicians, philosophers, and fortunetellers lived in the 6th century BC. He considered treatment his most distinguished mission. He described "pneumatics" or the energy associated with this process as the energy of light that appears around the body. After a hundred years, the famous Dr. Hippocrates insisted that the feeling of heat and sensations associated with the placing of arms and the transfer of energy lead to loss of pain. He tells the doctor to use energy, so we can assume that the doctors of ancient Greece have information about this practice.

In some European countries, the "touch of God" is intended only for the king, while in other countries monks can perform such healing methods. Later, many of these monks became innocent. In medieval Europe, there was a time when healing called "middle ground," which healed the disease and acted as the vehicle of god, was healed. Some people are considered "untouchables" because they act as a mediator or passage of God's energy. The Bible contains many explanations for the miraculous healing of the placing of arms. The healers of Christ and his disciples have experienced this conversion many times. Agreeing with those that follow traditions that are not Christian, such as "Taoism (China),

Buddhism (Tibet), Hinduism (India)," the healing procedure is determined by the conviction in the supremacy of the all-powerful essence of the world that pervades the entire creation. Each of us is a person with this mental element. More than this mystical component could aid other people to have a higher level of awareness.

In "Taoism" in the Far East, the use of qi (energy) for martial arts and healing is known. At first, only the "monks" in the monastery were acquainted with the notion of qi. Their time is full of prayer, meditation, and other diplomatic and modest events. Since they believe that including a background will aid uphold their flag and will enable communication with the essence of the omnipotent world. Neighboring hosts give food and pay for prayers. When thieves began to attack villages and temples, some monks decided to take active protective measures to sacrifice their monastic lifestyle and protect themselves from unwanted intrusions. During the battle, these monks use their ability to focus energy on their opponents, making it difficult to defeat them. This discovery led to the emergence of a martial arts school with a focus on defense, which eventually learned to use intense liveliness for attack drives. Another routine of liveliness is the curing of injured fighters. Often, it hurts in battle. To hasten the curing procedure, a fresh cluster of individuals has been designed, the supposed main pores, which can heal wounds with energy. The ability of this legendary qigong master to heal physical and mental pain has made them known for centuries. Today, China's new official name is people with special features. The energy released by the hand is used not only at the level of the body but also at all levels to restore proper energy balance and restore its integrity.

Legend has it that the defensive skills of the Shaolin monastery were considered a harbinger and developed after visiting the Bodhidharma, an Indian monk who paid attention to the poor health of the monks when they arrived at the temple. To advance his well-being, Bodhidharma educated him a sequence of liveliness maneuvers. As time went by, as the holy place grows and becomes more visible to attract thieves, an energy-based movement turns into a defensive training, turning into an offensive skill.

Handshakes have long been held by local shamans from the two zones. They will treat patients with the contact of hands and potions. This healing occurs only during the moon, when the moon grows, minimizing all healing actions when the moon decreases. (On all ancient continents, plants were harvested only during camouflage.) As part of healing rituals, local and African shamans dance almost unconsciously and bring their hands to sore spots on the body. Ancestors help to heal. In the two beliefs, melodic gadgets were used to generate definite pulsations and speed up the healing process. The indigenous people also draw dots and lines on the body that reflect the meridian (the passage through which energy moves), which the Chinese use for acupuncture!

For millennia, people of different cultures and beliefs have created a halo and mood round the skulls and statistics of people with "special powers," including healing supremacies. They go with Mary, Jesus's mother, and other essential Christian facts in the many ancient portraits, but people seem to be mistaken because they appear only around adult Christians. Christ as a doctor is usually showed not just with an aura and halo, similarly with light that originated in his arms. The Old Testament often remarks about the existence of brightness around other figures. In India and Tibet, you can see shining auras in the images of yogis, Buddhist monks, and all gods and goddesses. The Buddha is depicted not only by the energy around the body but by all the attributes in which the fully developed energy is depicted, that is, all the chakras (energy centers).

The head of the artistically crowned priest, warrior, and the leader of India represent a halo. Tibetans and Hindu mystics will demand this a completely established crown chakra or a thousand petal chakras.

Unluckily, these images of mortal liveliness fields have misplaced their principal significance over the centuries. John White shows 96 different cultures in his book Future Science. Despite the differences, each explanation shows signs of bright light or rays. Hello, their aura and all imitations symbolize originality and divinity and distinguish between those who have it and those who don't. But here is a fundamental variance amid the halo and other procedures of the crown. This circle is used to represent human virtue and good deeds and is a sure sign of spiritual development in all cultures. For crowns and other hats, the problem is often very different. Initially, the crown shows love, kindness, forgiveness, wisdom, and emotions, accompanied by high mystical growth.

In most of the olden customs, the primary connotation of the term "energy" is the original lifetime strength or liveliness of life. This liveliness seals and environs everyone and the environs. Rendering to this opinion of the world, the power of lifetime strengthens substance and generates natural life. In other arguments, natural life happens once liveliness enters nonliving substances. This natural life strength was famous as pneumonia in ancient Greece. "Paracelsus" called him a whale. In Sanskrit, in India, the term prana and mine, Prana means global liveliness, and mine is an individual procedure that streams over people and is distributed to schools of Bindu and Nibu. It is supposed that Prana can change the level of vibration and turn it into waves. In Tibet, this liveliness is known as Tikle, lungs, and Ca. In olden Egypt, it was known as "Ka." Chinese, the named Ki or Chi depending on the section of the republic. This last word comes from "tai chi" and qigong, the practice of meditative exercises based on the flow of energy. As mentioned earlier, anyone who can regulate and regulate the flow of energy is called a pore master.

Japanese, vital liveliness is known as "Ki." Its flow is used by "Aikido," schools offering martial arts and an active school of karate martial arts. In the United States, Japan's most famous energy tradition is Reiki.

The Hebrew text describes this authority as a lie. People should reflect four levels, three features of the Neshamah, Ruach, and soul-Nefesh. In Hawaii, this liveliness is known as "Mana and Ka," as in India, a human-level space vehicle is transformed into one or more aspects: what energy, what, that's it. "Mana or Ka" is cast-off for curing and self-regulation. The rulers of Hawaiian liveliness were known as kahuns. In Latin American nations, healers work with liveliness. The healer originates from the term "shams," meaning "sun" in olden Egypt, in Arabic and Hebrew. The solar is a source of energy on Earth and is worshiped in many ancient cultures.

Modern designations for this important liveliness consist of: "Odil (Karl von Reichenbach), Org (Wilhelm Reich) and Bioenergy (Professor Zdenek Reidak from Charles University in Prague, Czech Republic)." Since Kirlian began photographic experiments, many scientists who studied this subject were still engaged in this matter; another term was created in the former Soviet Union—bioplasma.

Today, it is becoming increasingly popular, as is Dr. Paul's approach to medical practice. Med. The sacred works of Randolph Stone and the skeleton of the Therapeutical Touch Technique, a liveliness management arrangement established by "Professor Dolores Krieger and Quantum- Touch Bob Rasmusson," are widespread with caregivers in the United States and several other nations. Bio vigor, by now is well recognized in Europe, extends to the United States. Far Eastern martial arts (exercises and vigor), these include "Aikido, Tai Chi,

Kung Fu, and Karate," are recognized worldwide. Due to the point energy pressure of the body, acupressure and shiatsu massage have gained popularity in spas and beauty salons. Qi Gong is located outside of China and is currently developing in the East and West. Should I consider this approach a medical act? Agreeing with the current description of the medicinal exercise, the response is no. Is there a relaxing effect? When I saw the results, they made it clear. Slowly found something missing in orthodox medicine.

A universal and energetic medication of the upcoming will certainly help from our experience in applying such procedures. Faced with fresh innovations, they will accept new interpretations that, unlike the past, do not put them in the category of magic or superstition. For clarity, the term "energy cure" is used in connection with functional outcomes obtained in electromagnetic, electrostatic, sperm or aural arenas, such as those cast-off for electrocardiography, electroencephalography, ultrasound, tomography and magnetic resonance imaging. This does not apply to the medical field X and more. The point that we expedition this device just endorses the presence of this field.

Many modern scientists conquer that in the universe, there is just one elementary system of vigor. At least from the point of view of the relativity of the magnetic field, this point of view is completely consistent with the point of view of occult energy. We believe that the universe in which we reside in, from spheres to stars, the sun, the astral system, and the galaxy, constantly vibrates, but most scientists do not even want to discuss spiritual energy. In addition, the Earth and all living things are in the same vibrational state as the cellular level. This vibration shows the vitality of the world. Conferring to this understanding, all flesh, comprising of human beings, is also liveliness beings. Most of our olden evolutions have known this for an extended time. This methodical information has been handed over from cohort to cohort in the Far East, India, Tibet, and China. As an invaluable fragment of the custom, this information is cast-off and used nowadays, and is also growing in popularity in other regions. There is no doubt that in recent years, part of this expansion is owing to the swift growth of studies that show and confirm the electromagnetic properties of a lifetime in the world.

Recent studies of the brain receptors, human, and brain waves, restrained at various levels of awareness, demonstrate the unbelievable possibility of self-regulation methods, as well as self-curing. Gradually, we began to understand the bigger fact that was removed in the period of reductionism. In utmost circumstances, a true cure for the disease requires more than just surgery or medication. You learn to give handy consideration to the entire physique, even if the delinquent happens just partially. We find that we feel better when we move the body, walk, breathe better, and spend more time in nature. We also know that what we eat and how to eat strongly affects our overall health. We take vitamins through a balanced diet and weight loss program, sometimes experimenting with fasting minerals.

Using this recent tactic, it was found that the whole physique is recovering, not the whole body or some organs. We are finally beginning to recognize the simple fact that organs and functions are not separated from other parts of the body. If it does not contain invisible components, such as our emotional, mental, and spiritual levels, the body should be considered and considered as a whole and incomplete system. There is no doubt that our feelings can kill or heal us and have a big impact on our health. In addition, we have no doubt that another inseparable reality, that is, our thoughts, dominates in our feelings. And our opinions and intents appear in a cerebral environ. The intention is the connection amid our cerebral and mystical levels. Our capacity of awareness decides the value of our intents, while our intentions and next steps represent our level of awareness.

The previously immeasurable self-healing potential that cannot be scientifically explained is clearly associated with our advanced levels of non-physical functions. In our desire to look good and survive extends or saves our lives, with the exception of many medical statistics and predictions from doctors. Representatives of homeopathic medicines often witness "voluntary relief" or "unexpected treatment." In many circumstances, these people will mask on a "diagnosis," and not admit that a miracle happened with the fact that the medicine they made cannot explain. Our ability to treat is rarely mentioned, and the ability to be treated by doctors is still mocked by the utmost customary doctors. The notion of remote treatment is deliberated very stupidly. This is completely incompatible with the paradigms of the past, but this skepticism is now seriously questioned by science itself.

What do you do with research based on scientific criteria (for example, double-blind) and showing affirmative variations in the focus's well-being when there is a doctor? More and more of these studies give very provocative results. For example, in the West Gulf of Medicine, Volume 169, Number 5, a study is published in which healers send energy prayers to Yatld to remote those sick with AIDS in "the San Francisco Bay area." The doctor and this patient not once saw each other or even talked to one another phone. But everybody must acknowledge that the variance amid the specimen cluster and other groups is very surprising.

Those that support the customary Western tactic to edification will only explain this as an occurrence showing that this result is an inexplicable event. This is not in line with the paradigm. Representatives of the culture of the Far East, on the other hand, will not be surprised at this result. They will understand that the energy in the form of prayer has been transferred to the spiritual level from afar. In the backgrounds, the precise flow of liveliness outside and inside our body is deliberated as an integral attribute of emotional, physical, spiritual, and mystical health. For those fascinated by this topic, see Ying Daniel Benor. Convincing evidence has been published on this subject, and many studies have been conducted on the country in which the study was conducted.

At the West, the conception of general liveliness medication or emerging vibrational medication is grounded on the supposition that people and the surroundings are made up of numerous systems of similar density. In a broader context, bioenergy is very compatible with this new drug model. This is such a procedure of skill as a medication of that period, which considers every person as a person and concerns the whole person, and not a specific service situation. Like creativity, bioenergy is based on vision, intuition, and art. There are definite instructions, but they should be free. It takes years of training and practice to be recognized as an artist or a doctor.

In a Chinese energy management system called qigong, internal and external energy flows can be slow, blocked, and weak or blocked due to damaged skeletons, broken or injured joints, damaged or broken nerves, meager movement, etc. Products that are too acidic or too basic (for example, too much yin or even in Chinese terminology), such as damaged skin or dirty, can cause an energy imbalance. We also get pretentious by demanding circumstances, when the nerve structure is not able to cope with tension correctly, and the electrical indicators in the head interfere with the stream of liveliness.

It processes the wrong flow of information when the flow of energy in the body is blocked, weak, or overloaded. As we are acquainted with, neurotransmitters regularly transmit data from the head to every cell and send data back as of each cell to the head. These "conversations," which take place in the form of information exchange in our bodies, occur beneath the surface of consciousness and are naturally biochemical and electrical. The mistake of "water supply" always bothers others. If this condition persists lengthier, the whole data structure in the problem zone is at risk. Cells misplace their capability to converse with one another and settle in the brain. Disorders that affect the stream of data through the physique has a similar consequence as the violation of data in new tissue systems. This will cause confusion and cause the system to crash. Now this incident, confusion repeatedly reveals itself as a disease. Thus, the disease could be initiated by a violation of the stream of liveliness in the physique.

The physique matrix could be considered to be a liquid or crystalline arrangement. There are many small tubes in this matrix that flow through the body. This tubule is commonly called the cytoskeleton. In fact, these are microfilaments observed at the subcellular environs, which are a fragment of a new-fangled vision that arises from the functions of the physique in "molecular biology." The dimension of the microfilament is four to six nanometers (imagine the regular granite and pay attention to the size: the marble faces the Earth at a speed of 1 nanometer per meter). This microfilament is present in every cell: it transfers proteins to specific targets, regularly moves organelles through cells, and even transfers RNA fragments beginning at the center to a precise conversion region. It is customarily believed that this microfilament or cytoskeletal collection plays a minor character in upholding cytoplasmic flow, cell integrity, and cell division. However, researchers recently recognized that the cytoskeleton is convoluted in signal transmission, molecular, and metabolism transportation of cells.

The base is the supposition that every breathing thing, including a human being, is bordered by general liveliness. We continue to receive energy from this sea, but each living creature has its own energy plan. Each relation amid breathing creatures involves an altercation of liveliness if we like it or we do not, whether we recognize it or not. Since we know the whole process better, we can learn more about ourselves.

Healing is an art that helps change the flow of energy to restore physical, emotional, mental, and spiritual health. Health-giving is a non-invading technique that can be used for all diseases, anxiety, or hurt. This is a medicine that has no recognized lateral properties and is equipped with every other treatment method. People can learn liveliness exercise skills to bring back the fitness and well-being of their own and that of other individuals.